MANAGING

STUDENT

EMPLOYEES

IN COLLEGE LIBRARIES

CLIP NOTE # 20

COMPILED BY

Michael D. Kathman
Director of Libraries and Media
College of St. Benedict/St. John's University

Jane McGurn Kathman
Professor of Management
College of St. Benedict

College Library Information Packet Committee
College Libraries Section
Association of College and Research Libraries
A division of the American Library Association

ASSOCIATION OF

COLLEGE

& RESEARCH

LIBRARIES

A DIVISION OF THE
AMERICAN LIBRARY ASSOCIATION

Published by the Association of College and Research Libraries
A Division of the American Library Association
50 East Huron Street
Chicago, IL 60611
1-800-545-2433

ISBN 0-8389-7752-9

TABLE OF CONTENTS

Miscellaneous

Employment/Dismissal

Job Descriptions

Applications

Interviews/ Reference Check

Employment Agreement

Dismissal

Orientation and Training

Orientation

Materials Handling

Training Checklist

Telephone Handling

Tests

Supervision and Performance Review

Supervision

Evaluation

CLIP NOTES COMMITTEE

Patricia Smith Butcher, Chair
Roscoe L. West Library
Trenton State College
Trenton, NJ

Carol Goodson
Ingram Library
West Georgia College
Carrollton, GA

Lawrie Merz
Willard Houghton Library
Houghton College,
Houghton, NY

Lewis Miller
Irwin Library
Butler University
Indianapolis, IN

Allen Morrill
Library
Kansas City Art Institute
Kansas City, MO

Karen Nuckolls
Lucy Scribner Library
Skidmore College
Saratoga Springs, NY

Elizabeth Sudduth
McGraw-Page Library
Randolph-Macon College
Ashland, VA

INTRODUCTION

Objective

The College Library Information Packet (CLIP) Notes program has been in existence since 1980. Its purpose is clearly explained by P.Grady Morein,

> The program provides college and small university libraries with state-of-the-art reviews and current documentation on library practices and procedures of relevance to them. The function of the CLIP Notes program is to share information among smaller academic libraries as a means of facilitating decision making and improving performance. The basic premise underlying the program is that libraries through out the nation are facing numerous challenges due to changing environments and that many of these libraries can benefit by knowing how similar institutions have resolved certain problems.[1]

This *CLIP Note* provides a new opportunity to look at the issues associated with managing student employees, updating *CLIP Note #7, Managing Student Workers in College Libraries,* published in 1986.

We have been offering CE 107: Managing Student Employees and variations of that course on a regular basis for over ten years. In teaching the course we have referred participants to CLIP Note #7. Much has changed since that time; there are a number of new laws as well as library issues that must be addressed now that were not concerns in 1986. As we taught the CE course we became aware of the great variation in the way different libraries and their institutions manage student employees. This CLIP Note is based upon a new survey recently completed by practicing librarians across the country.

Survey Procedure:

The procedures followed for this survey are the standard ones used by the CLIP Notes Committee. The survey was reviewed by the committee members and in March of 1994, surveys were sent to 260 small university and college libraries who agreed to be part of CLIP Notes surveys. The survey is based on our previous survey expanded to gather information on some of the new issues that have arisen over the past eight years. The responding libraries provided a wealth of sample documents, far more than could be included in this book.

[1] P. Grady Morein, "What is a CLIP Note?," *C&RL News* 46,5 (May 1985), 226.

SURVEY RESULTS

A total of 150 responses to the questionnaire were received, a 58% response rate. The tabulation of the results and the selection of documents was completed in the summer of 1994.

The complete results of the survey are included at the end of this section. What follows is a summary of the responses, highlighting the changes from our 1986 results, and comments on new areas of information.

Policies and Procedures (Questions 1-3)

It is clear that written policies and procedures are important to libraries, 76% of those responding have library specific policies and procedures in addition to institutional policies and procedures. This is a slight increase (from 74%) for student employees since our 1986 survey. The policies that are almost uniformly communicated continue to be: absence (96%), recording hours (90%), and responsibilities of general student work behavior (99%). Two policies that show a significant increase since our last survey are evaluation procedures from 56% to 62% and termination procedures from 47% to 69%. There was a slight increase in the percentage of libraries that have common policies and procedures for all departments from 73% to 79%.

Employment/Dismissal Process (Questions 4-16)

In a question new to this survey, only 61% of the institutions indicated they are required to hire "work-study" students over non-work study-students. There was an increase from 50% to 56% in the percent of institutions that use library-specific application forms. The most frequently asked information on applications forms was: class year (93%), skills (86%), hours available (83%), and previous work experience (81%). These responses were very similar to our 1986 survey. The application questions that showed the greatest change from 1986 to now (10% or greater) were: academic major (53% to 69%), available to work full year (29% to 39%), extracurricular activities (29% to 41%), hours per week of work elsewhere (14% to 28%), hours the student wants to work (69% to 47%) and skills needed (98% to 86%). There appears to be greater interest in finding out an employee's availability, extracurricular activities, hours worked elsewhere and ability to work the full academic year than in skills needed or hours the student would prefer to work.

In ranking the importance of the information on the application form, the top four items were: hours available, eligibility for work-study award (not used in the 1986 survey), availability to work weekends and nights, and availability to work the full academic year. The least valued information was academic major followed by extracurricular activities and grade point average. The major changes (.4 or more on a five point scale) between the two surveys are: academic major decrease of .67, availability to work holidays increase of .49, extracurricular activities increase of .74. Academic major is diminishing in importance and extracurricular activities and ability to work holidays is becoming increasingly important.

There has been no change in the percent of institutions that use pre-employment tests (22%). The final selection of student employees continues to be made by either the immediate supervisor or one individual who is responsible for hiring all student employees (90%). There is an increase in the number of immediate supervisors selecting their student employees (40% in 1986 and 53% now) and a corresponding decrease from 43% in 1984 to 37% in 1994 of the libraries having one individual responsible for all hiring. Students who do not perform their duties can be dismissed (97%), and if they are dismissed they can be replaced (94%).

In a new question we asked about dismissal procedures. The responses indicate that most institutions use a combination of verbal and written warnings. Some institutions include the work-study office, financial aid office, or the career counseling and/or placement offices in the process. In all institutions responding to this question, dismissal is a formal process where the reasons are made clear to the student employee.

Orientation and Training (Questions 17-25)

There has been almost no change in the percentage of libraries that give general orientation to their student employees (63% in 1986 and 64% now). The orientation sessions communicate to the student employees their importance to library operations (95%), general policies and procedures which relate to all student employees (91%), identification of where services and materials are located in the library (87%) and an introduction of library staff members (82%). This has changed very little since 1986. The same percentage (50%) as in 1986 include a statement of the library's goals and objectives as part of a general orientation. The immediate supervisor (85%) is the most likely person to do specific job training, but the use of experienced student employees in the area has grown from 13% in 1986 to 38% now. Less than half of the institutions (42%) provide students with individual departmental goals. Written training materials are provided by 74% of the institutions and 54% of the institutions test their training. More libraries are using computer assisted training (4% in 1986 and 14% now). The same program *Shelving Books the L.C. Way* is still the most popular program with one third of the respondents using it.

Supervision and Performance Reviews (Questions 26-37)

There has been an increase in the percentage of institutions that conduct performance evaluations from 63% to 70%. The frequencies of these reviews seems to be moving toward more being annual (from 43% in 1986 to 59% now). Written performance reviews are utilized by 90% of the responding libraries and 76% give the student employee an opportunity to make their comments part of the record. An increasing percentage of libraries (from 60% to 78% now) include a conference with the student employee as part of the evaluation process. The evaluations are made available to the student employees at 77% of the institutions, to the supervisors at 89% of the institutions, and to the work-study officer at 58% of the institutions. There continues to be little correlation between evaluations and pay (27% in 1986 and 28% now). Evaluations are used in conjunction with future hiring decisions at 87% of the institutions.

There has been a slight decrease in the use of student employees to supervise other student employees (from 32% in 1986 to 29% now.) Student supervisors receive a higher rate of pay 74% of the time, but they only have imput into the evaluation of student employees they supervise 26% of the time.

Miscellaneous (Questions 38-46)

There is no grievance procedure for student employees at 58% of the institutions. "Perks" for student employees are offered at 31% of the libraries. Two perks, no fines (57%) and parties/gifts (23%) are the most popular form. Differentiation between federal work-study and institutional student employment dollars continues to be the case at 80% of the institutions. This is down only 2% from 1986. Finally, it is interesting to note that the percentage of the library personnel budget that is spent on student employees has been in the 12% to 13% range in both surveys.

Selection of Documents

The responding libraries generously submitted many documents for our review. Due to space limitations we were unable to use many of them. In selecting documents we chose diverse samples from both large and small libraries which we felt were representative of all facets of managing student employees.

Conclusion

In comparing the current results with those of 1986, it is clear that the responding libraries are approaching the management of student employees more seriously. More libraries are using library specific employment application forms and there has been a significant increase in formal student employee evaluation procedures. Formalized termination procedures have been instituted at a large number of libraries. Finally, there has been growth in the use of experienced students training new student employees.

The responding libraries overwhelmingly continue to agree upon the importance of orientation sessions for student employees. Orientation topics of most importance are communicating to the student employees that they play a valuable role in library operations and general policies and procedures. The average number of full time equated student employees has changed little since 1986 (10.37 to 10.87 now), the head count has gone from 52 to 47.8 now, the average number of hours worked per week has decreased from 10.5 to 9.5, but the beginning pay rate increased from $3.35 in 1986 to an average rate of $4.51.

SELECTED BIBLIOGRAPHY

Childress, Schelley H. "Training of Student Assistants in College Libraries: Some Insights and Ideas." *Arkansas Libraries*. 44 (March 1987): 25-27.

Cottam, Keith M. "An Experience with Student Assistance." *Utah Libraries*. 12(Fall 1969): 24-27.

Coughlin, Caroline M. and Alice Gertzog. *Lyle's Administration of the College Library*. Fifth Edition. The Scarecrow Press, 1992. p 481-490.

Crawford, Gregory A. "Training Student Employees by Videotape." *College and Research Library News*. 49(March 1988): 149-50.

Frank, Donald G. "Management of Student Assistants in a Public Services Setting of an Academic Library." *RQ*. 24(Fall 1984): 51-57.

Fuller, F. Jay. "Employing Library Student Assistants as Student Supervisors." College and Research Libraries News. 51(October 1990): 855-57.

Fuller, F. Jay. "A Student Assistant Program for the Nineties." *College and Research Libraries News*. 48(December 1987): 688-692.

Guilfoyle, Marvin. "Computer Assisted Training for Student Library Assistants." *Journal of Academic Librarianship*. 10(January 1985): 333-36.

Kathman, Michael D. and Jane M. Kathman. "Integrating Student Employees into the Management Structure of Academic Libraries." *Catholic Library World*. (March 1985): 328-330.

Kathman, Michael D. and Jane M. Kathman. "Management Problems of Student Workers in Academic Libraries." *College and Research Libraries*. 39 (March 1978): 118-122.

Kathman, Michael and Jane M. Kathman. Managing Student Workers in College Libraries, *CLIP Note #7*. Association of College and Research Libraries. (1986)

Kathman, Michael D. and Jane M. Kathman. "Performance Measures for Student Assistants." *College and Research Libraries*, 53(July 1992): 299-304.

Kathman, Michael and Sherman Hayes. "The College Library as Guinea Pig: Student Projects on the Library. *College and Research Libraries News*, 53(October 1992), 572-574.

Lyons, Evelyn. "Student workers in the college library." In *Operations Handbook for the*

Small Academic Library, edited by Gerald B. McCabe, 91-8. New York:Greenwood Press, 1989.

McCarthy, Constance. "Paraprofessionals, Student Assistants, and the Reference Clan: an Application of Contemporary Management Theory. In *Academic Libraries: Myths and Realities*, edited by Suzanne Dodson ,382-86. Seattle: Association of College and Research Libraries, 1984.

Melnyk, Andrew. "Student Aides in our Library (Blessings and Headaches). *Illinois Library*. 58(Fall 1976): 141-44.

Rawlins, Susan M. "Technology and the Personal Touch: Computer-Assisted Instruction for Library Student Workers." *Journal of Academic Librarianship*. 8(March 1982): 26-29.

Richter, Anita T. "Student Assistants in the Library." *Catholic Library World*. (1978): 391-94.

Robertson, Ellen; Krismann, Carol. "Using Student Assistant Resources to Solve a Problem Creatively." *Colorado Library*. 13(September 1987): 25.

Shabel, Donald. "Performance Standards and Cost Analysis." *Illinois Librarians*. 64 (Spring 1982):875

Sichel, Beatrice. "Utilizing Student Assistants in Small Libraries." *Journal of Library Administration*. 13(Spring 1982): 35-45.

Vocino, Michael; Kellog, Martha H. "Student Employees in Academic Libraries: Premise and Potential." ED 301 220.

White, Emilie C. "Student Assistants in Academic Libraries: From Reluctance to Reliance." *Journal of Academic Librarianship*. 11(May 1985): 93-97.

CLIP NOTES SURVEY RESULTS

Library profile - FY 92/93: Averages from 150 responding institutions

Public 25   Private 125

1)	Number of FTE students enrolled:	2157.89
2)	Number of FTE librarians:	6.45
3)	Number of FTE's on library staff:	9.05
4)	Number of student employees (FTE):	10.87
5)	Number of student employees (head count):	47.80

Student Employee Questions:

1) Does your library have its own written Policies and Procedures to be followed by student employees in addition to institutional policies and procedures?

> YES   113
> NO   36

2) Which of the following policies and procedures does your library communicate to student employees: (143 responding institutions)

Responsibilities of general student work behavior	141
Absence policies	137
Recording Hours	129
Security procedures	104
Termination procedures	98
Rates of Pay	94
Evaluation Procedures	89
Dress Codes	72
Others (all are specific policies and procedures)	19

- Honor code; grievance procedures (2)
- Completion of training sessions, telephone policy, computer problems
- Promotion
- Submit semester class schedules
- Circulation manual
- Circulation training checklist
- Orientation
- Processing and circulation procedures
- Safety
- Procedure manuals and work directions
- Communications
- Reference letters for potential employees

3) Do all departments in your library have common policies and procedures?

> YES   117
> NO   31

4) Are you required to hire "work-study" students over non-work study-students?

> YES   88
> NO   56

5) Who determines the rate of pay?

Institution   130
Library   24
Supervisor   12

6) In the selection process does your library use an application form for student employment in your library?

> YES   83
> NO   64

7) Which of the following do your ask for on an application form? Please check all that are applicable:

Class year (First year, Sophomore, etc.)	84
Skills (computer, AV, etc.)	78
Hours available to work (or class schedule)	75
Previous work experience	73
Previous library work	71
Academic major	62
Eligibility for "work-study" award	56
Availability to work weekends, nights	53
Areas of the library where he/she would like to work	42
Hours the student wants to work (preferred hours)	42
Extra-curricular activities	40
Availability to work full academic year	35
Course load for semester-number, difficulty of classes	35
Hours per week of work elsewhere	25
Recommendations	25
Grade Point Average	25
Availability to work holidays	21

Others (please list)   18
- Name, address, phone number of student (4)
- Why do you want to work in the library (4)
- Foreign language (3)
- Social security number
- Personal statement
- Can you drive a vehicle with standard transmission?
- Can you carry heavy equipment across campus?
- Interview
- Class schedule
- Expected date of graduation
- If transferred from another school
- Grade in last English/typing class
- Willingness to sub for other assistants

8)   On a scale of 1-5 with 1 being most important and 5 least, how would you rate the
      value of the information you receive on the application form? (94 responses)

Average Rating	Number of Responses	
1.7	81	Hours available to work (or class schedule)
1.82	65	Eligibility for "work -study" award
1.95	60	Availability to work weekends, nights
2.00	51	Availability to work full academic year
2.47	51	Hours the student wants to work (preferred hours)
2.53	60	Skills (computer, AV, etc.)
2.65	74	Previous library work
2.67	60	Previous work experience
2.69	48	Recommendations
2.73	55	Hours per week of work elsewhere
2.82	53	Areas of the library where he/she would like to work
2.84	76	Class year (First year, Sophomore, etc.)
3.02	43	Grade Point Average
3.06	52	Extracurricular activities
3.12	42	Course load for the semester
3.21	42	Availability to work holidays
3.67	63	Academic major

Other:
-       Knowledge of foreign languages (6)
-       Transferred from another school (5)
-       Grade in last English and typing class (2)
-       Date of graduation (2)

- Science majors are usually the best student workers
- Name and address of most recent employer
- Name, address, and phone number of student

9) Does the library administer any tests that are given to the student applicants?

YES   33
NO   114

10) If a test is used, who "grades"the test? (32 responses)

- Supervisor (25)
- Staff member (2)
- Librarian (2)
- Training team
- Library student employment coordinator
- Self-graded in a group

11) If you use a test, what are the criteria for "passing/failing?"

- Cannot fail--generally used as a measure to assess knowledge of the job and what areas need to be reviewed and practiced. (8)
- Test is arranging call numbers in order; "mostly right" passes. (3)
- They cannot file or shelve until they pass test to satisfaction of supervisor to new students--this is a big deal.
- I would consider 1 or 2 missed questions as all right-- more than 4 would be failure.
- Used each term for current employees--discussed with supervisor to encourage proper work.
- Ability to learn, understand basic Library of Congress system, using a written explanation with flash cards and "test" books to be shelved.
- Must demonstrate mastery of content.
- Must get all answers correct.
- Ability to follow directions, readability of answers.
- Comprehension, accuracy, degree of difficulty in completing test.
- Must take class - Library Orientation, IM 101 for 1 credit and pass with a B- or better (may audit class with same criteria).
- Test is used as a learning aid. It is taken after a week's training to look for gaps in their knowledge. At a later point, the test is taken again with no aids.
- Ability to score at least 60% on "LC Easy."
- 90% correct.
- Purpose to check mid-semester on policies/procedures.
- If they miss more than 3, we don't hire them.
- 70% accuracy before allowed to reshelve books.

- Problem areas are discussed with students; if the student had a problem area, that is worked on and tested again.
- There is no pass/fail designation. One unit gives a call number "quiz" during the interview, after explaining filing rules. Quiz is used to determine trainability, whether student has aptitude or is hopelessly confused by decimals. Other tests may be used to determine need for additional training in specific areas.
- Quality of work.
- We get a "feel" for whether the student is detail-oriented, sloppy, careful, etc.--allows us to pick the better ones there is not pass/fail.
- Ability to recognize call numbers and respond to call number exercises.

12) Who is responsible for the final selection of student employees? (148 responding institutions)

- The immediate supervisor	79
- One individual in the library who is responsible for hiring all student employees in the library	55
- Each department head in the library	46
- Campus student employment office (or other non-library office)	28
- Other (please list)	2
Library director	
Immediate supervisor and library director	
communal library supervision	

13) If student workers are sent to you by a campus student employment office, are you required to hire them?

YES   13
NO   132

14) Can you dismiss students who do not perform?

YES   141
NO   4

15) If yes, what are the procedures for dismissal? (After written notice, formal hearing, etc.)

There were 137 responses to this question, with many variations as to the combination of written and verbal notices. Listed below are sample responses that introduced variables that might be of interest.

- Counseling with the work-study supervisor, followed by special instruction. Termination follows continuance of incompetence or non--compliance with instruction.
- Written notice to employment office; hearing with student; conference with student and supervisor.
- Written notice of unsatisfactory performance is turned in to institution's work-study supervisor, who reassigns the student.
- We just tell them they are not working out and invite them to seek campus employment elsewhere.
- Documentation of grievances; counseling with student worker in the hope of improvement; joint counseling with supervisor; department head, and student worker; notification of campus student employment office of termination.
- Some actions mandate immediate dismissal.
- Two weeks' notice to student and notification to the financial aid office.
- A written notice of the problem signed by both supervisor and student. The third such notice is automatic termination.
- Written notice sent to Career Counseling and Placement office.
- After a period for probation, if performance remains unsatisfactory, notice explaining the reasons for probation must be given to the employee and a copy sent to the Financial Aid Office.
- Usually this is a mutual decision between the supervisor and the student. If necessary we will send the student back to financial aid saying we think they would be happier working somewhere in the College other than the library. Then it's financial aid's problem.
- Done very informally.
- When hired, they sign "condition of employment" sheet. If they don't show up, they are usually told I'll fire them next time. If there are other problems, they are given three warnings in person and in writing. If they visit too much, they are encouraged to work someplace else.
- Probation letter, review, on training or counseling, then one more warning.

16) If you answered yes to question 14, can you hire replacement students?

           YES   138
           NO   9

17) Does the library have a general orientation for student employees?

           YES   90
           NO   60

18) Which of the following does your general orientation contain? Please check all that are applicable. (101 responding institutions)

- Communicate to the student employees their
  importance to library operations   96
- General policies and procedures which relate to all
  student employees   95
- Identification of where services and materials are
  located in the library floor plan   89
- Introduction of library staff members   83
- Welcoming the new employees   74
- Telephone etiquette   65
- Statement of library's goals and objectives   50

- Others   19
    - training on automated circulation system (4)
    - security measures (2)
    - How to use OPAC (2)
    - Need to police library--for noise, eating/drinking, animals, and watch for book damage and plates cut out of art books
    - Video for student employees
    - Brief description of work of each department, refreshments
    - Copy machine maintenance, reserve materials, making change
    - Stacks maintenance and preservation
    - Hands-on experience throughout library
    - Discussion of log book - used for communication between supervisor-student and student-student (ex. "Can someone work for me, etc.)
    - Most view <u>Murder in the Stacks</u> and <u>Enemies of Books</u> (Two videos on preservation/how to handle books).

19) Who is responsible for specific job training? (Check all that apply) (147 responses)

Immediate supervisor   125
Experienced student employees in the area   56
Department head   53

Other (please list)   13
- Other full time library employees (2)
- Assistant circulation manager
- Assistant media canter manager
- Public services department librarian
- Director
- College does some general training for work-study students
- Media, technical services, ILL

- Student managers
- Training team
- Student coordinator
- Library secretary/desk supervisor

20) Do you provide student employees with individual department goals during training?

YES 60
NO   83

21) Are student employees provided with written training materials and/or handbooks to refer to in the future?

YES 111
NO   39

22) Are the results of your training tested?

YES 73
NO   63

23) If you answered yes to question 22 do you use: (75 responding institutions)
(Check all that apply)

Results of work	63
Paper/pencil test(s)	31
Oral test(s)	18
Computerized tests	10
Other (please specify)	6

- Check list is used for stack maintenance. As students master skills or jobs, it is noted.
- At one month, we review what procedures they feel inadequate with.
- Verbal reviews and updates on any changes.
- Individual hands-on practice with shelves and cabinets for proper shelving of books, periodicals, and microfiche. Results checked for accuracy.
- Informal feedback.
- Practical demonstration by student to show ability and knowledge to use automated system.
- Reference Department.

24) Do you use computer-assisted instruction to help train student employees?

YES   19
NO   121

25) If the library answered yes to question 24: (18 responding institutions)

a) Please list any "commercial" programs that you use and the computer needed to run the programs. (16 responses)

- *LC Easy* (c 1991, Mary L. Kish); DOS; EGA or VGA Graphics Display; IMB memory; 3.5" 1.44 MB Diskette drive (High Density); printer (6)
- shelving books the LC way: A self test - Apple IIe, LC Easy - IBM (2)
- LS 2000, Sc 350, ACQ350, OCLC, UMI, CD ROM Package, various library networks
- Data Research (DRA) for Circulation Services (software)
- CLC IU Training
- Software tutorials run on personal computers
- YNIX Automated Library Systems
- "Library Stacks" from the University of Tennessee Libraries
- "Call Number Order" by Calico Publishing (Apple)

b) Please list the topic areas and computer needed to run any programs designed by you or your staff. (5 responding institutions)

- Hyper card stack for media desk, hyper card stack for circulation desk
- Various
- Apple II GS--covers the LC and Dewey # systems, how to shelve books, maps of the library
- Circulation/reserve, periodicals, acquisitions, cataloging, processing
- Library stacks modified to suit our individual libraries

26) Does the library conduct performance evaluations for student employees?

YES   103
NO   45

(If you answered no to number 26, skip to number 35)

27) If the library evaluates individual student employees, how often are the evaluations scheduled? (106 responses some more than once)

Annually   63
Each term   43
Other   10
    - 6-week evaluation, then annually
    - Bi-annually
    - Twice per month
    - Every two months
    - As need arises
    - Brief monthly evaluations on student payroll vouchers
    - Monthly basis
    - Ongoing

28) If the library evaluates individual student employees, are these evaluations in writing?

YES   97
NO   11

29) If the answer to 28 is yes, are student employees provided the opportunity to have their comments part of the record?

YES   73
NO   23

30) If the library evaluates individual student employees, is part of this process a conference with the student being evaluated?

YES   82
NO   23

31) If the supervisor does not have a conference with the student being evaluated, do you communicate the results of the evaluation in any other way?

YES   29
NO   39
(if yes, please explain briefly)

- Student gets copy of evaluation. (8)
- Student is shown written evaluation and asked to sign it, indicating that he/she has seen it. If student wishes, discussion is possible at this time. (2)
- If student is unavailable for a meeting, I send a copy of the written evaluation to the student and request their comments. (2)

- At the rehiring of each term and establishment of the next term schedule.
- They are sent to Office of Career Development to remain with their personnel records, which the student may review.
- Inappropriate work habits are discussed with student when behavior occurs or as soon as possible after the incident.
- Serials/ILL: if student has worked up to standards and beyond, they will be asked back for the following semester. If not, problems will be discussed and student hired back on a "probation" status.
- Main Desk: students who perform very well are told they are doing a good job by the Main Desk supervisor. Those who are not are given goals to achieve; if they do not, they are dismissed.
- Reference letter put in seniors' placement files.
- Written form.
- Evaluation interviews are held by immediate supervisor of student assistants during April. The evaluation form (provided by Financial Aid Office) is used during the interview. Both student and supervisor sign the form. Original is sent to Financial Aid Office. A copy is kept by the supervisors only if a student is not able to come for the interview--over a period of time--until the supervisor fills out the form.
- Written on evaluation.

32) If the library does written evaluations, who sees the evaluations? Check all that apply. (100 responders)

Student employee's supervisor	89
Student employee	77
Work-study officer/financial aid officer	58
Library director	42
College Personnel Service	15

Other (please list)   12
- Public Services Librarian (2)
- Department Head (2)
- Administrative asst. - Dean's office
- Circulation supervisor
- Student assistant supervisor
- 2 individuals in charge of student employment
- Student coordinator keeps a copy of all evaluations
- Career planning and placement
- Associate Public Services Librarian
- Library Director's Executive Assistant
- Copy for student job references upon request

33) If the library evaluates individual student employees, does the evaluation have any relationship to rates of pay?

YES 30
NO 77

34) Are evaluations used in conjunction with future hiring decisions?

YES 93
NO 14

35) Are student employees used to supervise other student employees?

YES 42
NO 101

If so, check areas that apply.

- Circulation   37
- Media   12
- Tech Services   10
- Reference   7
- Administration   0

- Other (please list)   6
  - reserve desk (2)
  - Government Documents (2)
  - Stacks
  - Library extension
  - Preservation

36) If yes, do they receive a higher rate of pay?

YES 32
NO 11

37) If yes to question 35, do they have input into the student employee's evaluation?

YES 11
NO 31

38) Does the library have a student grievance procedure?
Check all that apply. (139 responding institutions)

- At the institutional level	36
- At the library level	31
- None are available	8

39) Does your library offer any type of "perks" to student employees?

YES 46
NO 101

40) If yes, please check those that apply and/or are applicable to your library. (44 responses)

- No library Fines	25
- Free Database Searching	6
- No fee ILL	6
- Free Photocopying	5
- Free FAXing	3
- Other (please list)	20

- Parties, gifts (10)
- Incentives given for years of service
- Bonus (1.25) during exam week. Increased pay level for opening/closing library and higher skill level of work.
- Promotion to office jobs; more pay and responsibility
- $.10 per hour raise per year of service, Christmas pizza party
- Selection of work hours and movement to different jobs
- Senior luncheon, Christmas treats, Brunch
- All students have extra-special advice on reference work
- Reference help while working
- Specialized BI
- Semester study carrels
- Student appreciation activities:
- Student Assistant of the Semester/Year Award; Senior Tea; Senior Gifts, etc.
- Student of the month gift certificate
- At the end of term this spring an award of $40.00 gift certificate to the campus bookstore to the outstanding student employee.
- They have the use of office machines
- First choice of carrels, flexibility of hours, housing and lunches during holidays and summer, end of semester party
- Christmas party, senior gift (Atlas or book)

41) Does your institution differentiate between federal work-study dollars and institutional student employee dollars?

YES   112
NO   28

42) If you answered yes to question 41, are students allocated to the library based on: (119 responding institutions)

- Library budget   65
- Library needs   81
- The need to find jobs for all students   29

- Other reasons (please explain)   5

  - Take any student that applies, fill remaining positions with our budget federal work-study funding.
  - Federal work-study funding.
  - Distribution of student labor based on institutional funding.
  - Quota determined in Financial Aid.

43) What are the dollar amounts spent on student employees annually? (Averages)

FY 91/92 $58,299.20
FY 92/93 $56,462.09
FY 93/94 (budgeted) $61,807.88

44) What percentage of the library personnel budget (including benefits) was spent on student employees? (student employee budget divided by all library employees, including student employees)

FY 91/92   13.25%
FY 92/93   12.83%
FY 93/94 (budgeted)   12.58%

45) What are the average number of hours worked each week by individual students during the normal school year (exclude summers)?

Average hours worked = 9.52

46) What was the average hourly rate of pay for student workers in FY 92/93?

Average pay rate = $4.51

POLICIES AND PROCEDURES

Handbooks

Emergency Procedures

Miscellaneous

Hollins College

STUDENT ASSISTANT HANDBOOK

FISHBURN LIBRARY

1993-1994

WELCOME

Fishburn Library's primary objective is to provide positive public service to students, faculty, staff and the College community. **YOU** are a very important part of this operation.

YOU represent the LIBRARY to all our patrons. You, your attitude, and your eagerness to help will influence the patron's view of our library. Please take your work as seriously as we do.

MISSION STATEMENT

The mission of Hollins College Fishburn Library is to provide information, services, and programs which meet the education, research, and public service needs of the College community.

YOU WILL MAKE A DIFFERENCE!

Each of you will spend many hours working in the Library this year, serving patrons and completing transactions. Every time that you assist a patron, you project the impression of an efficient and friendly library. Your performance **will** make a difference!

Your position warrants a great deal of respect from all of us at Hollins. You work demanding hours on weekends and evenings in addition to hours between classes. You also have to deal with pressures from fellow students, faculty and staff.

Many students choose to continue their work in the library for more than one year. It can be a valuable experience for you. The library recognizes that **you** are very **important** in assuring an efficient operation **and** in making the library a pleasant place to work.

You do make a difference!

FISHBURN LIBRARY
BASIC JOB EXPECTATIONS FOR
STUDENT EMPLOYEES

RELIABLE ATTENDANCE:

* Arrive on time.
* If ill, notify supervisor.
* **You** are responsible for arranging a replacement.

INITIATIVE:

* Do priority work first.
* Perform additional tasks.
* Offer suggestions for improvement.

RESPONSIBLE ATTITUDE and BEHAVIOR:

* Take job seriously.
* Perform work accurately.

POSITIVE ATTITUDE:

* Accept assignments willingly.
* Cooperate with others to achieve mutual goals.
* Contribute to a pleasant work environment.

ADHERENCE TO LIBRARY POLICIES AND PROCEDURES:

* Read the departmental policy and procedure manual.
* Always consult supervisor before making exceptions to general policies.
* Never discuss confidential library matters with non-staff.

GOOD SERVICE:

* Always provide good, positive service
* People before paperwork
* Be available, identify yourself, and offer assistance
* Always be pleasant - no matter how busy you are

"You're welcome" is a wonderful phrase - use it often!

HELPFUL HINTS TO FOLLOW

- Be responsible, arrive on time.

- Comply with work schedule.

- Be friendly, smile, show interest, and look approachable.

- Professional ethics - Do not discuss patron or staff matters with non-library personnel.

- Studying allowed ONLY after patrons are served and tasks are completed, contingent upon supervisor's approval.

- Keep social conversation brief.

- Keep service desk area neat and uncluttered.

- Encourage users to ask questions.

- Never keep patrons waiting.

- Our success depends on YOUR positive attitude.

COMMUNICATION

Team work and effective service depend upon good communication

- Make sure that you understand specific tasks. Please ask questions.

- Before leaving, either tell your supervisor or leave an explanatory note as to task progress.

- Encourage questions. If uncertain of answers, refer to appropriate staff or leave a written message if staff is unavailable.

- Brief your supervisor on any problems that occur during your shift.

- Use sound judgement when making decisions. Consult with a staff member if uncertain.

Hollins College

CHANGES IN WORK SCHEDULE

You may be required to work some evening and/or weekend hours. You may schedule your times in minimum two hour blocks. You are responsible for working the number of hours agreed upon with your supervisor. Changes in your schedule need to be discussed with and approved by your supervisor.

Students working in A/V or the Circulation Department must find a trained substitute.

In case of illness, call to report your problem :

Acquisitions	-	6241	ILL	-	6592
Audio Visual	-	6383	Periodicals	-	6239
Automation	-	6082	Reference	-	7465
Cataloging	-	6235			
Circulation	-	6591	Library Dir.	-	6232
Gov't Docs.	-	6241	Secretary	-	6240

EXAM TIME

This is a busy time for you and the Library. It is also an excellent time to make up any hours that you may have missed due to illness. We will reschedule work hours around your exams.

TIME CARDS AND PAYROLL

Student pay vouchers are located in the Circulation Department. Vouchers will be in alphabetical order and will be processed monthly.

To avoid delays in payment please be sure that you sign your pay voucher.

Please fill out the number of hours that you work. If you work 4 or more hours per shift, you are entitled to a 15 minute paid break. Please arrange this with your supervisor. Also, please arrange any meal time breaks with your supervisor, and deduct the amount of time taken from your hours.

TINKER DAY

Fishburn Library will be open on Tinker Day. If you are scheduled to work during the day and are climbing the mountain you are excused. **If you are not climbing, you are expected to report for work at your assigned time. If you are not climbing and would like to work extra hours, check with your supervisor. Please report for work if you are scheduled when Tinker Day officially ends.**

COLLEGE CLOSURE

What do I do if the college is closed due to emergency weather conditions?

We will make every attempt to keep the library open and we ask for volunteers to help us in this endeavor. Please let your supervisor know if you would like to be part of the Emergency Library Crew.

GROUNDS FOR DISMISSAL

We have tried to make clear our expectations for our student staff. It is your responsibility to read and understand the "Grounds For Dismissal" policy. If you have any questions concerning this policy, please consult your supervisor.

A.   You as a student assistant may be dismissed for any of the following reasons:

1. Refusal to do assigned tasks and/or insubordination.
2. **Frequent** tardiness from work without prior permission from your supervisors, or three unexcused absences.
3. **Unauthorized** use of library facilities, materials and/or supplies.
4. Improper reporting of hours on time card.
5. Consistently poor job performance.
6. Failure to consistently maintain a positive service, oriented approach toward patrons, staff and co-workers.
7. Reporting to work under the influence of alcohol or other illegal substances.

B.   Failure to comply with one or more of the listed expectations will generally be handled in the following manner by your supervisor:

1. Verbal Warning

2. Written Warning

3. Dismissal

A supervisor may bypass step one and proceed to step two if circumstances warrant.

C.   If overall performance rating is marginal and after significant warning there is no improvement, you will not be rehired for the subsequent semester.

D.   There is an appeal process for a written warning. You may appeal in writing to the head of the Department or the Library Director if you feel that the warning was unjustified.

PERFORMANCE EVALUATIONS

You are responsible for the quality of your work. Performance evaluations are completed towards the end of each year. You and your supervisor will have the chance to discuss your strengths and weaknesses and decide on objectives that will help your overall effectiveness.

BASIC CRITERIA FOR PERFORMANCE EVALUATION

ATTENDANCE

* Arrives on time.
* Dependable work schedule.
* Notifies well in advance of schedule conflicts.

ATTITUDE

* Shows interest in work.
* Willingly receives and carries out instructions.
* Seeks performance improvement.

COMMUNICATION

* Listens carefully.
* Provides accurate information.

JUDGEMENT - INITIATIVE

* Ability to adapt to changing situations and procedures.
* Analyzes and uses sound judgement.
* Shows resourcefulness and initiative.
* Plans and organizes work.

OBSERVES POLICIES

* Adheres to library policies and procedures.

PUBLIC SERVICE

* Sensitive to patron's needs.
* Gives correct and complete information or refers patron to appropriate department.
* Represents library in a positive manner.

PRODUCTIVITY

* Follows task to completion.
* Strives for greater efficiency.
* Uses time wisely.
* Generates acceptable or above standard rate of work.

QUALITY OF WORK - JOB KNOWLEDGE

* Accurate, neat and dependable.
* Attention to detail.
* Keeps work area clean and well organized.
* Knowledge of procedures.

RESPONSIBILITY

* Meets job demands with minimal supervision.
* Attention for care of supplies and equipment.
* Accepts responsibility for own decisions.

TRAINING OTHERS - LEADERSHIP

* Provides motivation and guidance .
* Explains instructions clearly.
* Follows through on trainee's work until acceptable level is attained.
* Takes charge of situation when necessary.

WORKING RELATIONSHIPS - COOPERATION

* Acknowledges the difference in working and social relationships.
* Cooperative attitude toward students and staff.
* Accept suggestions and criticism as well as praise.
* Works well on cooperative projects.

DACUS LIBRARY
WINTHROP UNIVERSITY
Rock Hill, SC 29733
1989/90
Revised January 1990
Revised June 1990
Revised August 1991
Revised August 1992

STUDENT EMPLOYEE HANDBOOK

Student Employee/Orientation Committee

Winthrop University

Table of Contents

Welcome

We are very pleased that you have joined the library staff. Dacus Library could not function without your assistance. You may be surprised to learn how working here will not only benefit you with work experience, but will also teach you how to use the library effectively in your studies. In the pages that follow, you will find general information about your job and information about library policies. We always welcome your questions.

Dacus Library Staff

Winthrop University

The Purpose of this Manual

This manual has been prepared to give you an understanding of what you can expect from us as faculty and staff, and what we, in turn, expect of you as student employees.

Since this manual cannot cover in detail the specific jobs you may find yourself having to do, each department will have its own procedure manual in addition to what is given here.

We are grateful for the hours of work you contribute as student employees. What the faculty and staff are trying to do is to make your work experience at Dacus Library a positive one, and also to prepare you for a job in the career world. We want to encourage you to work for a high scholastic average which, coupled with a good job record, will be very valuable to you in the future.

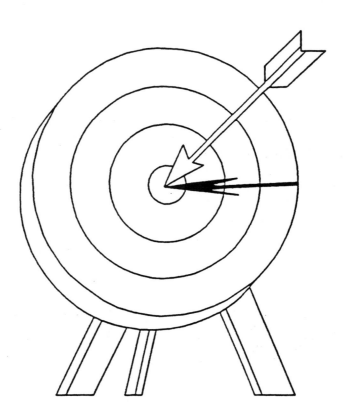

Introduction

Dacus Library depends on a large number of student employees to assist the library staff in the daily operation of the library. Although some library tasks may seem routine, such as searching, labelling, or shelving, these tasks, completed correctly, help provide quality library service to your classmates, friends and professors. Working in the library as a student employee is not "...just a job" or "...something I have to do to get work-study." Working at Dacus Library is a commitment of time. If you are to be a successful employee, you must learn to exercise your time management skills from the beginning. If you are scheduled to work just prior to a test, you will need to figure out when to finish your studies ahead of time. While you are a student first, you are also a library employee and need to honor your obligations here. We believe that the better you balance your study and work time, the better you will be able to manage other areas of your life. Student employees are an important part of the Dacus Library organization and the staff appreciates your contribution.

Benefits of working as a student employee in Dacus Library
---flexible hours
---transportation not needed by most students
---valuable work experience
---learning to be an important part of an organization
---learning how to use the library
---graduated pay scale

A Dacus Library student employee
---is responsible
---reports to work when scheduled
---notifies supervisor when unable to report to work
---has a positive attitude
---limits socializing during work hours
---asks questions
---takes assigned library tasks seriously
---can be trusted to work unsupervised
---is courteous to supervisors, other student employees
   and library users
---smiles! remembers to say "please," "thank you," and "you're welcome."

Winthrop University

Each of you will work out your schedule with, and be instructed in your duties by, the supervisor for whom you will work. Also, there are several general matters of which you should be aware and for which you must assume responsibility. If you have questions, discuss them with your supervisor.

ORIENTATION: All student employees are required to attend a brief orientation to be held at the beginning of the fall semester (clock in when you arrive and clock out when you leave).

TIME CARDS: Clock in and out using your own time card each work period. You will be paid for the completed work periods which show on your time sheets. You must sign your time sheet between noon on payroll day and 4 p.m. the next day EVEN IF YOU ARE NOT SCHEDULED TO WORK DURING THAT TIME. (A list of the pay periods and paydays is posted on the time clock.) YOU WILL NOT BE PAID UNLESS YOUR TIME SHEET IS SIGNED. If you make an error punching your time card, see your supervisor.

EMPLOYMENT: You must reapply for campus employment each year and summer session. Contact the Financial Resource Center regarding work-study awards and apply for other library positions at the Student Employment Office (Personnel Office) 1 Tillman. In order to work and receive a paycheck, you must have signed I-9 and W-4 forms and been approved to work by the Student Employment Office or the Financial Resource Center.

FALL/SPRING BREAKS AND HOLIDAYS: Student employee weekly hours are calculated to include only the time school is in session. Fall/Spring breaks and holidays are excluded. Therefore, student employees are not expected to work during breaks and/or holidays. However, those who desire to make up time previously lost may work during these times. Prior approval from immediate supervisor must be obtained.

BREAKS: If you work three or more hours consecutively you are allowed a fifteen-minute break. DO NOT clock out, just be sure to inform your supervisor before leaving and when returning. Student employees are not allowed to use the staff lounge or staff restrooms because of the size of the facility and the number of people on the staff. Breaks cannot be used to cover a late arrival or early departure.

FOOD OR DRINK: Student employees are not allowed to have any food or drink in work areas.

DOORS: Student employees must use the front doors to enter or leave the library (fire exit or back doors may not be used).

 TELEPHONE: Do not make or receive phone calls during working hours. The staff answering the phone will be glad to take messages. A telephone is available in the second floor lounge which you may use on your break.

SOCIALIZING: Do not socialize with your friends while at work. Tell them you will see them when you finish working.

JOB ATTIRE: Since student employees contribute to the image of the library, you are to maintain a neat and clean appearance and to be appropriately dressed. Tattered or distracting clothing should not be worn.

 STUDYING: NOT ALLOWED WHILE WORKING--NO EXCEPTIONS.

ELEVATORS: An elevator is available for employees to use while on duty. Priority is given to the handicap patrons.
Patrons are encouraged to use the steps instead of the elevator.

WEEKENDS: The librarian on duty at the Reference Desk at night and on Saturday and Sunday is in charge of the Library.

EMERGENCIES: Report any emergency, such as fires, leaks, floods, medical emergencies, etc., to the staff person on duty. If you are on duty alone, call the Public Safety Office (extension 3333) immediately.

PROBLEM PATRONS: If you observe a patron in the library who appears to be "suspicious" or is abusive towards someone or toward any library materials, obtain a complete physical description of the person and inform a library staff member. If you are on duty alone, call the Public Safety Office (extension 3333).

Hiring, Evaluation and Disciplinary Action

Hiring

Students seeking employment in the library must apply at the Student Employment Office (SEO), located in the Personnel Office, 1 Tillman. The SEO maintains application cards of students who are interested in working on-campus. Student employee positions which are available are posted by the SEO on a bulletin board in the corridor outside the Personnel Office.

When there is a vacancy to be filled in the library, the Administrative Specialist in the Dean's Office fills out a Job Vacancy Notice for Winthrop Student Employees Form for each student required by departments. This form is sent to Student Employment where the positions are posted. The Student Employment staff screen the applicants and send over several for the library staff to interview. Once the interview is complete, students are notified of the hiring decision by telephone or mail. Students are hired based on their qualifications (skills and experience) in relation to the needs of the hiring department. Each department has job descriptions for all student employee positions.

Students employed during the summer session are hired for summer only. If the position he/she worked during the summer is vacant in the fall, this student will be given first priority because of the training received during the summer. Students who leave for the summer, after being employed during the spring semester, can usually be reappointed to the payroll if they return to library employment in the fall. The supervisor should inform the student of the possibility for fall employment and the deadline date for contacting the library. DUE TO THE UNCERTAINTIES OF FUNDING, HOURS, ETC., NO STUDENT CAN BE GUARANTEED LIBRARY EMPLOYMENT. Any prospective student who fails to contact the Library before the deadline date will no longer be considered for employment by the library.

Each student hired with library funds must fill out an Hourly Wage Agreement Form, an I-9 Form (Immigration and Naturalization), and a W-4 Form. The prospective student employee, the Administrative Specialist, and the Associate Dean of Library Services must sign the Hourly Wage Agreement Form before submitting it to the Student Employment Office for approval. Once approved, the student can begin work.

The University Work-Study Program is a federally-funded program designed to create jobs for those students who need to work in order to attend college. Work-study students are approved and assigned to the Library by the Financial Resource Center. All work-study students must also fill out an I-9 Form and a W-4 Form. NO STUDENT EMPLOYEE IS ALLOWED TO BEGIN WORKING UNTIL APPROPRIATE FORMS HAVE BEEN FILLED OUT AND PROPER SIGNATURES OBTAINED.

Probation and Dismissal

Student employees are employed on an introductory trial period for one month. At the end of that month, the supervisor evaluates the employee's performance and determines whether he/she will be able to fulfill the work requirements or whether dismissal is warranted.

After the initial trial period, any student employee who violates work attendance regulations or instructions

Winthrop University

will be warned by his/her supervisor. (Note: Warnings can be imposed on any student employee by library personnel other than his/her immediate supervisor.) Only one verbal warning will be given.* If there is no satisfactory improvement concerning the conduct in question, then a written warning (Appendix A) will be issued to the employee by his/her supervisor. The written warning will list the reason(s) for the warning, citing specific problems and necessary changes. This will also be noted on the reverse side of the time card for that time period.** A REPEAT OF THE VIOLATION(S) IS CAUSE FOR DISMISSAL. The employee will not receive any more warnings after the written warning prior to employment termination.

Violations that mandate warnings and possible dismissal include (but are not limited to) the following:

1. refusal to do assigned tasks
2. unauthorized use of university or library equipment (i.e., typewriters, using photocopiers for personal work, computers, etc.)
3. inappropriate use of work time (i.e., personal phone calls, socializing, homework, etc.)
4. disrespect for supervisors, other student employees, and/or library patrons
5. failure to work scheduled hours
6. unsatisfactory work performance
7. failure to provide a substitute in your absence (if required by your supervisor)
8. sleeping while on duty
9. reporting to work under the influence of alcohol or a controlled substance

Violations that mandate <u>immediate dismissal</u> (but are not limited to) are:

1. failure to report to work within three days after classes begin
2. falsification of time card records
3. theft
4. willfully causing damage or destruction of equipment or property belonging to the University, students or other employees.

Supervisors are encouraged to confer with department or division heads before issuing a written warning to or discharging a student employee.

 A student employee MUST notify his supervisor of his desire to terminate employment, stating reason.

A formal evaluation (Appendix B) of your performance will be made at the end of the first semester and at the end of each spring semester thereafter and upon termination of your employment in the library.

---

*A supervisor may bypass the verbal warning and proceed immediately to a written warning if circumstances warrant.

**The student employee will sign the warning sheet, and it will be filed with his/her evaluation form in the Office of the Dean.

Work Schedules

Students are expected to report to work by 4 p.m. the first day of classes and must report no later than 4 p.m. the third day of classes. STUDENTS WHO FAIL TO REPORT TO WORK WITHIN THREE DAYS AFTER CLASSES BEGIN WILL BE TERMINATED.

Work schedules will be set up when student employees report to work. Student employees are urged to fill out a reasonable schedule, so that absences will be minimal.

Student employees must finalize their work schedules no later than two weeks after classes begin. Changes after that time must be justified.

Student employees should work their approved schedules. Any deviation from these schedules requires supervisor's permission.

Student employees must fill out amended work schedules as soon as the exam week schedules are announced.

Student employees who have been absent from work must schedule makeup time with their supervisors.

Student employee must notify his/her supervisor as soon as possible PRIOR to the scheduled work time if he/she cannot report to work. Failure to notify your supervisor will result in a warning. Failure to notify your supervisor a second time warrants dismissal. You are strongly advised to place the phone call yourself and speak with your supervisor or other departmental personnel.

On-campus students are asked to report during inclement weather, unless the Library is officially closed.

Student employees are given raises based on their work performance and the length of time employed by the library. The hourly pay rate is as follows:

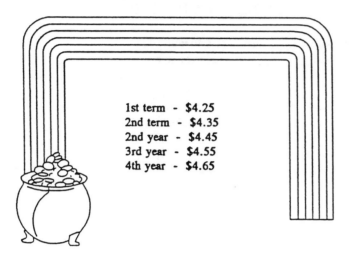

1st term - $4.25
2nd term - $4.35
2nd year - $4.45
3rd year - $4.55
4th year - $4.65

There are two pay periods per month—first through fifteenth and sixteenth through the end of the month.

The Administrative Specialist sends payroll sheets to the Payroll Office on the first and sixteenth of each month. (If this falls on Saturday or Sunday, payroll is then submitted on the following Monday.)*

 Time sheets must be signed by the student employee between noon the day of payroll and 4 p.m. the next day EVEN IF YOU ARE NOT SCHEDULED TO WORK DURING THAT TIME. Time cards are pulled after 4 p.m. if sheets are not signed. If you do not sign your time sheet by payday, your check will be held—only released once the time sheet is signed.

Paychecks are issued on the tenth and twenty-fifth of each month by the Payroll Office. (If this falls on a Saturday or Sunday, then checks are issued on the previous Friday.)*

Student employees must pick up their paychecks in the Payroll Office, 21 Tillman. (In some cases, students go to the Cashiers Office to sign their checks over to the University.) If a student employee needs his/her check mailed to his/her home, a form must be filled out in the Payroll Office before payday.

---

*The Payroll Office may change dates during holidays and breaks. Changes will be posted on the time clock.

Library Organization

Administrative Structure

Administration Office
    Dean of Library Services
    Associate Dean of Library Services
        Head, Public Services Division
        Head, Technical Services Division

Public Services

Circulation Department
Reference
    OnLine Searching
    ILL (Interlibrary Loan)
    Bibliographic Instruction
    Government Documents
Archives

Technical Services

Monographs Acquisitions Department
Monographs Cataloging Department
Serials Acquisitions and Cataloging Department
Preservation and Bindery Unit
Access Control Unit

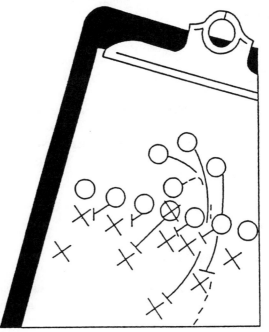

Departmental Functions
(in order as presented above)

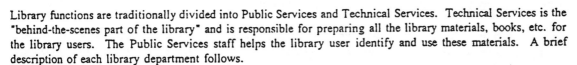

Library functions are traditionally divided into Public Services and Technical Services. Technical Services is the "behind-the-scenes part of the library" and is responsible for preparing all the library materials, books, etc. for the library users. The Public Services staff helps the library user identify and use these materials. A brief description of each library department follows.

ADMINISTRATION

The Dean of Library Services is responsible for the supervision of all aspects of library operations, which includes library policies, programs and budget, in consultation with the university administration, the university faculty and the library staff. The Dean is assisted by the Associate Dean, the Heads of Public Services and Technical Services. The support staff of the administrative office handles general administrative office routines, payroll, supplies, etc.

PUBLIC SERVICES DIVISION

Circulation Department

The Circulation Department maintains the library collection and provides circulation services to the library patron. Books are checked out, renewed and checked in at the circulation desk. The Reserve collection is located at the circulation desk. If a library patron cannot locate a book or a book is checked out, they can request the book at the circulation desk. The staff maintains the Vendacoder and Mita copiers and collects all incoming library monies, such as overdue fines and lost book charges. Student employees in the circulation department assist the staff with circulation services at the circulation desk and maintain the library collection by shelving, shelf-reading, shifting and straightening in the stacks. The Circulation Department's main goal is to provide quality service to the library patrons.

Reference Department (main floor)

The main goal of the Reference Department is to assist patrons in locating the materials needed for their research purposes. Students assigned to work in the Reference Department maintain the Reference collection, file updated material in the loose-leaf services located in reference, help organize and reshelve in the vertical files, photocopy needed materials for the department and perform other various miscellaneous tasks as assigned.

Within the Reference Department there are different units. A student may be assigned to work specifically within one of these units.

Online Searching (Reference Office)

This unit is responsible for searching national and international databases to produce subject bibliographies. This unit is also responsible for the CD-ROM indexes in the Reference area.

Interlibrary Loan (Reference Office)

This unit is responsible for borrowing books and magazine or journal articles not owned by Dacus Library, from other libraries for our patrons' research needs. Dacus Library also will loan books and articles to other libraries requesting these materials. Student employees working with this unit are responsible for processing material in and out of Dacus Library, and for maintaining the Interlibrary Loan files.

Bibliographic Instruction (classroom and office on bottom floor)

This unit is responsible for library instruction, including lectures in upper level classes tailored to the research requirements for the class assignment, as well as a "hands-on" type approach for all the Writing 101 classes. Student employees working with this unit are responsible for producing, maintaining, and cleaning the packets of materials required for the classroom presentations.

Government Documents (top floor)

Dacus Library is a U.S. designated depository library for federal and state (South Carolina) publications. Student employees working with this unit are responsible for shelving and reshelving government documents and microfilm materials, processing materials, copier maintenance, as well as performing other duties as assigned.

Archives and Special Collections (ground floor)

Archives and Special Collections houses: the inactive records created by various departments and offices on campus; the personal papers of alumni, faculty, staff, and friends of the university; records relating to the history of the Catawba region; material relating to the history of women in South Carolina; Winthrop University theses; oral history tapes; rare books and other special materials.

TECHNICAL SERVICES DIVISION

Monographs Acquisitions Department

The Monographs Acquisitions Department is responsible for ordering and receiving all the books and audiovisual materials for the library collection. Gifts, replacements, and the paperback collection are also handled by this department. The staff verifies order information received from faculty and librarians, orders, receives and processes materials, and monitors the book budget. Students help verify order information, type order cards, and process materials.

Monographs Cataloging Department

The Monographs Cataloging Department is responsible for cataloging, classifying, and preparing for the shelves books and audiovisual materials. This department also maintains the public catalog as a comprehensive index to most of the materials in the library. Student employees in this department can work with one or more computer systems.

Serials Acquisitions and Cataloging Department

The Serials Acquisitions and Cataloging Department orders serial publications, checks-in serial issues as they are received, and prepares serial issues for the current shelves or for the general collection, and claims missing issues. It also takes care of the current periodical shelves, and catalogs serial publications in order to make the title, author, and subject information for each serial title accessible to the students, faculty, and staff of Winthrop University, and updates the information on the "List of magazines, journals, and newspapers in Dacus Library."

A serial publication is anything published with the intention of being published indefinitely. This includes newspapers, magazines, annual publications, etc.

Binding and Preservation Unit

The Binding and Preservation Unit is responsible for planning, monitoring and coordinating the development and preservation of the library's collections. All activities relating to commercial and in-house binding and mending are performed by the Binding staff.

Access Control Unit

The job of the Access Control Unit is to make the Dacus Online Catalog (DOC) as useful as possible for library users. Student employees in this area work with Library of Congress documentation, computer generated reports and two computer systems in the verification and correction of subject, author, and title headings.

Winthrop University

DACUS LIBRARY
STUDENT EMPLOYEE WARNING/DISMISSAL SHEET

NAME:_____ DATE: _____

DEPARTMENT:_____ WARNING:_____ DISMISSAL:_____

VIOLATIONS THAT MANDATE WARNINGS AND POSSIBLE DISMISSAL:

_____ unauthorized use of university or library equipment (i.e., typewriters, photocopiers, computers, etc.)

_____ inappropriate use of work time (i.e., personal phone calls, socializing, homework, etc.)

_____ disrespect for supervisors, other student employees, and/or library patrons

_____ failure to work scheduled hours

_____ unsatisfactory work performance

_____ failure to provide a substitute in your absence (if required by your supervisor)

_____ sleeping while on duty

_____ other (please specify) _____

VIOLATIONS THAT MANDATE IMMEDIATE DISMISSAL:

_____ failure to report to work within three days after classes begin

_____ falsification of time card records

_____ theft

_____ willfully causing damage or destruction of equipment or property belonging to the University, students or other employees

_____ other (please specify) _____

COMMENTS:_____
_____
_____

_____   _____
Supervisor's Signature   Date   Department/Division Head Signature   Date

****

By signing this form I am certifying only that this form has been shown to me. The fact that I have signed this form should not be interpreted as either agreement or disagreement.

_____
Student Employee's Signature   Date

44 - Policies and Procedures

APPENDIX B

DACUS LIBRARY
LIBRARY STUDENT EMPLOYEE PERFORMANCE EVALUATION
INSTRUCTIONS

PURPOSE: An annual evaluation of student library employees is performed to provide the employee with an indication of his or her performance and to provide the Library with a record for purposes of rehiring and provisions of employment references when requested.

1. Evaluation will be performed at the end of the student's first semester of work and at the end of each spring semester thereafter and upon termination of employment of each student employee. Additional evaluations may be performed by the supervisor as needed.

2. Completed evaluation will be available to the student employee for inspection and signature.

3. Completed evaluations are confidential and may not be inspected except as provided by law. Student may give blanket permission allowing potential employers access to this form. The evaluations will be filed in the Dean's office.

4. Person performing the evaluation should attempt to be as accurate as possible and not "overrate" or "underrate" a student employee.

    Exceeds expectations - significantly and consistently performs at level above that expected. Achieves results beyond most people at this level.

    Meets expectations - meets major requirements; is consistently effective and competent. Achieves results expected from people at this level.

    Fails to meet expectations - work is overall unsatisfactory. Improvement possibilities questionable.

5. Heading portion should have a computer label affixed and characteristics should be checked in ink.

6. Comments should be included whenever necessary for clarification or when printed comments do not completely reflect a student employee's performance.

7. It is anticipated that this form will be revised as experience dictates.

8. Anyone outside the Library staff who views the completed form must fill out the section below.

Name   Reason   Date

_____

_____

_____

CONFIDENTIAL

I hereby give permission for any potential employers who are investigating my employment record to have access to this form.

_____   _____
Signature (Student Employee)   Date

Winthrop University

C O N F I D E N T I A L
LIBRARY STUDENT EMPLOYEE PERFORMANCE EVALUATION

AFFIX LABEL:

_____

Year_____

BRIEFLY LIST DUTIES PERFORMED BY STUDENT EMPLOYEE:

_____
_____
_____
_____
_____
_____

_____

Attitude--cooperative, conscientious, pleasant _____
Responsibility--attendance, is dependable_____
Promptness_____
Cooperation--works well with others _____
Efficiency--quality of work, accurate, thorough _____
Mastery of Job Skills--learning the job _____
Need for supervision _____
Productivity--quantity of work _____

Supervisor's Comments:

_____
_____
_____
_____

General Rating: Exceeds Expectations ____ Meets Expectations ____ Fails to Meet Expectations ____

Would you rehire yes _____ no _____

Supervisor Signature _____ Date _____

Student Employee Comments:

_____
_____

Employee Signature _____ Date _____

By signing this form I am certifying only that the rating indicated on this form has been shown to me. The fact that I have signed this form should not be interpreted as either agreement or disagreement with the rating given.

46 - Policies and Procedures

IV. EMERGENCIES

In most cases, a staff member will be available during an emergency to direct Student Workers in assisting. There will, however, be occasions when Student Workers are working without staff supervision and will need to know how to respond to an Emergency situation.

Elmira College Emergency procedures are included in this packet and are posted near the phone. In addition, the following procedures should be followed for GTL emergencies.

1. Fire. In case of fire, pull the fire alarm and call the Fire Department. GTL fire alarms are local, that is, they only sound here, not at fire headquarters. Once the Fire Department has been reached, call Security.

Once emergency services have been contacted begin evacuating the building.

2. Accident or Illness. Call emergency medical services directly using the numbers on the EC Emergency Procedures sheet.

In medical emergencies, once emergency services have been contacted, also call the Clarke Health Center in case there is a qualified person on duty there who might be of assistance. Once emergency services have benn contacted, call Security.

Do not attempt to move a victim or administer assistance unless you have proper training in the appropriate procedures.

3. Bomb Threat. Call Security. If Security can't be reached, call the City Police directly and once they have responded, continue trying to reach Security.

Record the time of the call and the content of the message and await the arrival of emergency personnel. Once emergency personnel arrive, follow their instructions.

4. Threatening, suspicious or disruptive patrons. Any patrons who are being unusually disruptive or reports of patrons engaged in activity that is supicious or that could be considered illegal or threatening, including theft, should be handled by Security. If you observe a situation or receive a report, call Security immediately. If Security can't be reached, call the City Police and once they have been notified, continue trying to reach Security.

A patron making a report of such activity should be asked to wait at the Circulation Desk with you until Security or the Police arrive. If the offending patron leaves before Security arrives take note of his or her characteristics so that they might be identified later.

Do not attempt to deal directly with anyone you perceive as threatening or potentially criminal.

Occidental College

It is Occidental policy to provide a safe and healthful workplace for all employees. To that extent, the College has implemented the Injury Prevention Program.

Members of management are expected to do everything within their control to ensure a safe environment and to always be in compliance with federal, state, and local safety regulations.

Employees are expected to obey basic safety rules as outlined below, follow established safe work practices and exercise caution in all their work activities.

All employees are expected to immediately report any unsafe conditions to their supervisor. Employees at all levels of our organization who are qualified for correcting unsafe conditions should do so.

Working together, the College can succeed in having a safe and healthful workplace from which we all will benefit.

BASIC SAFETY RULES

1. All injuries must be reported to your supervisor immediately.
2. You are encouraged to take an active interest in your own safety by developing good work habits and bringing unsafe working conditions to the attention of your supervisor and the Campus Safety Officer.
3. Good housekeeping is essential for preventing accidents. Keep your work area clean and free of trip, fall, slip, and laceration hazards.
4. Personal protective equipment **must** be worn or used in any area where it is required. Do not alter or disable existing safety features of equipment.
5. Be aware of the location and the use of first aid kits and fire extinguishers.
6. When personal safety and equipment are involved, there are no "dumb" questions. Always ask your supervisor if you are in doubt about how to operate a tool or perform a task. Do not operate a tool or machine for which you have not been completely trained on.
7. Established job procedures must be followed by all employees. Changes in regular job procedures require the approval of your immediate supervisor.
8. Use only the proper tool for the job. Do not use defective tools or equipment. If the proper tool is not available, get help from your supervisor before doing the job.
9. Get assistance in lifting any item which is so bulky, awkward, or heavy to move that you feel it is unsafe or unhealthful, and report it to your supervisor immediately.
10. If a repetitive task causes you discomfort, or you feel it is unsafe or unhealthful, report it to your supervisor immediately.
11. Alcohol and other non-prescription drugs are prohibited in the workplace.
12. Injury prevention is our goal, however if an accident or near accident should occur, immediately report it to your supervisor and follow all the proper reporting procedures.
13. If you have any questions call the Safety Officer at ext. 2933.

I have viewed the Occidental College Library Safety Video and have read the above information outlining the College's Injury Prevention Plan.

NAME _____

SIGNATURE _____ DATE _____

EMERGENCY PROCEDURES-- October 1992

☎ ALWAYS CALL 9-911 immediately for **fire** or **severe illness/injury**

☎ ALWAYS CALL SECURITY x711 FIRST (if no answer, try x358 or 361)
Security will make the other necessary contacts. This number is also accessible in a power
outage (see Power Outage below for other accessible phones).

→ **Building supervisors** are responsible for implementing any emergency procedure
needed within their building. For Dunn Library, Cyd is the building supervisor (home 961-
2104), Mike is backup supervisor (961-7250) and Kristi is Mike's backup (961-4853).
   ☎ STAFF/STUDENTS: With an evening/weekend crisis, call security and use your best
      judgement. Call Cyd ASAP. Do not hesitate to contact the building
      supervisor/backup if you are ever questioning a situation.

✚ SEVERE ILLNESS/INJURY
Call 9-911 for paramedics and notify building supervisor.

▌ POWER OUTAGE
An emergency flashlight is plugged into the outlet by the lockers in the circulation office.
Administrative staff should remain in their offices.
With an evening/weekend outage, call the building supervisor or backups for instructions. If no
   one is home and lights remain out for over thirty minutes, close the library.
If the outage involves the phone system and you need to make a call or receive a call, the
   following phones close to the library will still work: College Hall, Heidi Raymond, x693;
   Barker Head Resident, x426; Kresge Head Resident, x261.

❄ SNOW
Even if classes are cancelled, the library should remain open if at all possible. (This is also
   true of food service, Cowles Center, McNeill Lab and the student center.)
With an evening/weekend snowstorm, call the building supervisor or backups for instructions.

● FIRE/EARTHQUAKE
Know where the fire alarms and fire extinguishers are located (map attached).
If there is a fire, pull the nearest fire alarm to notify those in the building.
Enlist someone to call the fire department (9-911).
Evacuate people from the building as long as there is minimal risk to your safety.
Leave through the front door (first choice) or through any available emergency exit.
All library staff should meet in the northwest corner of the Barker parking lot.
Use this same meeting spot if there is an earthquake.

● TORNADO/SEVERE STORM
In the event of a tornado (town siren will go off), tornado warning or severe storm, occupants
   should get away from the large glass windows and go to the first floor microcomputer lab
   or the northwest stairwell, lowest level (enter on second floor)(first choice) or Kresge
   basement (second choice).

→ **BOMB THREAT**
If you receive a call, remain calm. Get the supervisor or, if no one else is here, obtain the following yourself: location of bomb, time of detonation, reason for threat. Evacuation decision will be made by the supervisor.

☎ **CRIMINAL ACTIVITY**
Call Security (x711). Depending on the situation, you may need to call the police (9-911).

* * *

☎ **CAMPUS CRISIS CENTERS:**

Information Center: 0 (or x701-710, 712-715, 493), Red & Gold Room, College Hall
> In the event of a campus-wide crisis, people may contact this center for information about the crisis.

Volunteer Center: x531, Commuter Lounge, Hillman Hall
> In the event of a campus-wide crisis, students and staff should report to this common pooling area for assignments, identification passes and information.

Student Verification Center: x667, Career Services, Brenton Student Center
> In the event of a campus-wide crisis, people may contact this center to get information about specific students.

President's Crisis Command Center: x490, President's Conference Room, Hillman Hall
> In the event of a campus-wide crisis, the President may call together his crisis committee to coordinate efforts, make decisions and provide information for the media.

Procedures for Dealing
With Attempted Theft

When you observe someone trying to steal materials or behaving suspiciously, ask the person to come to the circulation desk. If the person

Doesn't Stop	Do not attempt to physically stop the person yourself or ask others others to stop him/her. Report the incident to your supervisor and record the incident in the Security Log. Include a description of the person and where she/he was last seen.
Stops	Ask him/her to come to the Circulation Desk. Do not accuse the individual of attempting to steal library material. Notify your supervisor and ask the person to stay at the circulation desk until your supervisor arrives.

Supervisor's Procedures

Record and report incidents to campus police for the following situations:

-- A person triggers the alarm and responds "No" to a request to inspect his/her belongings.

-- It appears that library materials have been deliberately concealed.

-- A person runs through the exit and triggers the alarm.

__ A person who is acting suspiciously at the exit, e.g., hands over head, tossing materials through exit, etc.

-- A person refuses to give you information about him/herself, e.g., name, address, telephone and SS numbers.

Technical Services Staff
at Card Catalog

If the alarm sounds and a person exits without returning to the circulation desk, do not attempt to stop him/her. Get a description and report it to Carmen or a librarian.

If you observe a person acting suspiciously around the exit gates notify the librarian in charge or circulation staff. Do not confront the person yourself.

Our Lady of the Lake University

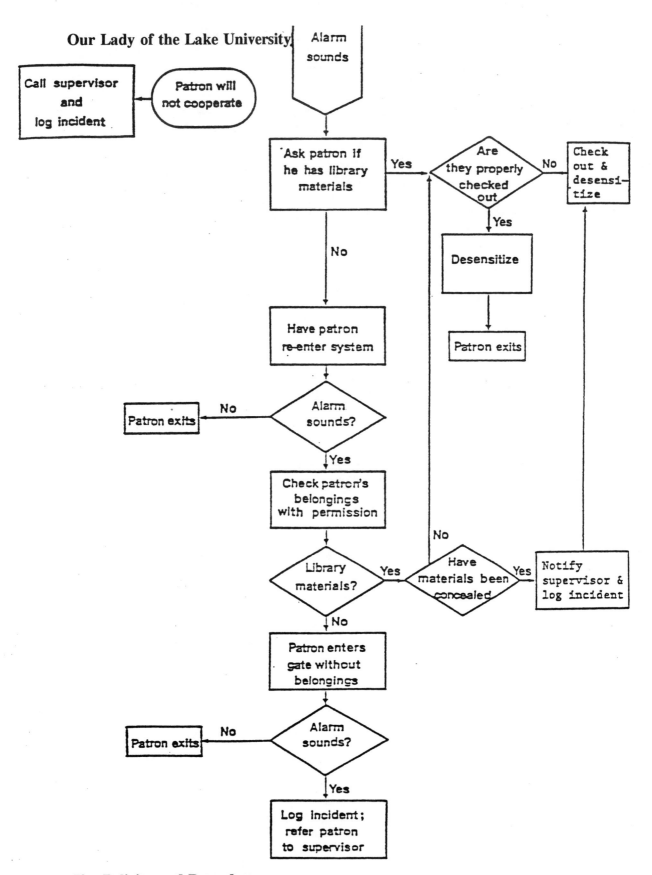

MEMORANDUM

TO: Library Student Workers

FROM: Library Office (bd)

SUBJECT: NEXT OF KIN INFORMATION

I have requested that this information be kept on file so that in case of emergency we know who to notify.

Please complete the following information and return to me as soon as possible. Married people please list next of kin other than spouse (to be notified if spouse is not available). Single people list persons other than roommates.

YOUR NAME:

HOME ADDRESS:

HOME PHONE:

SPOUSE'S BUSINESS PHONE:

PERSON OTHER THAN SPOUSE TO BE NOTIFIED IN AN EMERGENCY:

Name

Address

Phone

ALTERNATE TO NOTIFY IF ABOVE CANNOT BE REACHED (optional):

Name

Address

Phone

EMPLOYMENT/DISMISSAL

Job Descriptions

Applications

Interviews/Reference Check

Employment Agreement

Dismissal

ADAMS STATE COLLEGE LIBRARY

Position: Circulation Desk Attendant

Description: The Circulation Desk Attendant is the first contact person for most patrons who enter or call the Library. In a businesslike manner, the Desk Attendant performs circulation activities for patrons, directs patrons to appropriate library staff for other services and acts as telephone receptionist for the Library.

Requirements: Current Adams State students, generally work study, who are service oriented, accurate about detail, prompt and dependable. Typing skills are required, and some computer experience is preferred.

RESPONSIBILITIES

The Circulation Desk Attendant is accountable to the Circulation Supervisor on duty for efficient performance of the following tasks:

1. Arrives promptly and dependably at scheduled times and remains at the desk until relieved.

2. Knows and performs all circulation and reserve procedures for students, faculty and other patrons in a friendly manner.

3. Answers incoming telephone calls in a friendly manner and transfers calls to appropriate staff or takes legible, accurate messages.

4. Returns all materials deposited in the book return drop boxes and places returned materials in designated area for re-shelving.

5. Counts and files all manual circulation cards left from the previous shift.

6. Arranges for a substitute to work in the event of absence due to schedule conflicts or illness. Promptly reports absence and substitution arrangements to Heidi Heersink (589-7782) or supervisor on duty.

7. Maintains a businesslike environment in the circulation area by not using the telephone for personal calls, not visiting with friends and not listening to music while on duty.

8. Performs other tasks as assigned by supervisors.

Transylvania University

Transylvania University Library

JOB DESCRIPTION

Title: Circulation Student Assistant

Reports to: Circulation Supervisor and/or Night Supervisor (depending on
                hours scheduled)

General duties: The Circulation Student Assistant performs circulation-
related activities at the Circulation Desk and assists library patrons to
utilize the facilities, collections and services of the staff and
librarians. The Circulation Desk is the principal point of contact between
the patron and the library. Therefore, the first impression of the library
and even the campus as a whole is that which the Circulation Student
Assistants project. Circulation Student Assistants are responsible for
staffing the Circulation Desk for up to 16 hours a day, providing
directional assistance to patrons, and referring patrons to a librarian for
reference assistance.

Specific responsibilities:

I.   Efficient performance of general circulation desk duties including:

     A. Circulation

         1. Knows and performs all circulation and reserve procedures
             for students, faculty and special patrons in a friendly,
             knowledgeable and service-orientated manner.

         2. Collects overdue fines.

         3. Maintains drawer change, makes change for vending machines
             and transfers excess money to Circulation Supervisor's
             office.

         4. Signs auditrons for copiers in and out, assists patrons with
             the correct use of the machines, adds paper when needed, and
             records copier charges accurately.

         5. Maintains a neat and orderly appearance at the Circulation
             Desk, in the book drop area, the shelving area, and with
             current newspapers.

         6. Implements the use of the electronic security system when
             checking books in or out, and by addressing the patron when
             the alarm sounds.

B. Collection maintenance:

    1. Reshelves books.

    2. Shelf-reads assigned collection on a weekly basis to keep the collection arranged in exact call number order and easily accessible to patrons.

II. Support of general operations:

A. Knows all librarians and staff and their functions in order that proper referrals can be made.

B. Knows how to make proper referrals.

C. Knows the location of individual library areas and can define the use of each so that patrons can be directed appropriately.

D. Answers telephone with correct telephone protocol.

E. Performs correct opening and closing routines when scheduled at the beginning or end of the day: doors, lights, copy machines, clearing building of patrons from all areas of the library including ground floor study rooms and rest rooms.

F. Maintains order and a quiet atmosphere proper to the library environment, especially when Student Assistants are on duty alone.

G. Assists in keeping the library neat and orderly at all times while on duty.

III. Participation in special projects as directed by the Circulation Supervisor or one of the librarians such as photocopying projects, moving books in the stacks, inventories, checking bibliographies against the catalog, or other assignments.

IV. Observance of library policies as outlined in the "Employment Agreement." In particular:

A. Arrives promptly when scheduled, reports scheduling conflicts or illness promptly to the Circulation Supervisor and arranges and reports substitutes by use of the "Student Substitute Form."

B. Dresses appropriately and is well-groomed.

C. Refrains from talking with friends or making personal telephone calls while on duty.

D. Communicates verbally or in writing problems encountered during an assigned shift, or any other information that might provide helpful knowledge for library staff.

E. Reads notices in Circulation Supervisor's office and at circulation desk daily.

F. Keeps accurate time cards.

Union College   STUDENT JOB DESCRIPTION

DEPARTMENT:_____BLDG:_____

DEPARTMENT HEAD:_____

STUDENT SUPERVISOR:_____

POSITION TITLE: Government Documents Student Assistants_____

NO. OF STUDENTS REQUESTED FOR THIS POSITION:__2_____

DESCRIPTION OF DUTIES:

Opens federal depository shipments (5-10 boxes per week); stamps and verifies

receipt of publications in depository shipments; shelves & files newly-received

documents in both paper and fiche formats; shelves & files documents used in-house

or circulated returns; files USGS topographic maps; other projects as assigned

(e.g. security stripping, filing cards and shipping lists, shelfreading,

searching for lost documents, shifting to make room where shelving is tight,

labeling and checking in hearings, etc.); some special projects

QUALIFICATIONS AND SPECIAL SKILLS:

Thoroughness, accuracy and attention to detail are paramount, also reliability

and initiative. Patience and persistence are also qualities that come into play

for the portions of this job that become repetitive or routine. Computer and/or

typing skills are helpful and neat, legible handwriting or printing are needed.

Some physical strength for lifting and shifting may be called for.

SIGNATURES:

DEPARTMENT HEAD:_____   DATE:_____

STUDENT SUPERVISOR:_____   DATE:_____

HAVERFORD COLLEGE LIBRARY JOB APPLICATION

Please note:
This application form is for those who have never worked for Magill Library before. Returning employees should contact their supervisors directly.

Please Print or Type

I.   General Information

1. Name _____   2. School / Class _____

3. Major _____   4. Work Study? (circle one) YES / NO

5. Mailing Address _____

6. Campus Phone _____   E-mail user name _____

7. Home Address _____

_____

Home Phone _____

8. Reference _____

II.   The Fun Part -- Show Time

1. Work Experience _____

_____

_____

2. Special Skills (including computer skills, language ability, talents or interests)

_____

_____

_____

_____

3. Tell us something about yourself: your personality, your dreams or any reasons you
   think we should hire you

_____

_____

_____

_____

_____

_____

_____

Haverford College

III.   Down To The Business

1.   How many hours can you realistically work each week? _____

2.   Preferred position(s) at the library:

                                      (1) _____

                                      (2) _____

                                      (3) _____

****

For Official Use Only

Date received _____

Interviewed _____

Refer to _____
Hire? yes / no
Added to payroll? yes /no

STUDENT LIBRARY ASSISTANT
JOB APPLICATION

Date:_____

Semester applying for (circle one): Fall   Spring   Summer   19

Name_____Social Security Number_____

School Address_____School phone_____

Home Address (include town):_____

_____

Current status (circle one):   FR   SO   JR   SR   Major_____

Birthdate_____   G.P.A. _____

Work experience (any part or full time):

EMPLOYER	POSITION

Have you worked in a library before (include school libraries)?:
Yes_____   No_____   If yes please describe the work you did:_____

_____

_____

Have you taken the Library Research class? Yes_____ No_____
Have you taken and passed the proficiency test? Yes_____ No_____
Are you JMS? Yes_____   No_____.
If you answered NO to all the above, when will you take the
class? _____

Are you employed elsewhere during the school year? Yes_____ No_____
How many hours per week? _____
Is the job on Millikin's campus? Yes_____ No_____ Where?_____

Approximately how many hours a week did you want to work?_____
Can you work evenings? Yes_____ No_____
Can you work weekends (at least alternate weekends)? Yes_____
No_____
Can you type? Yes_____ No_____. Approx. W.P.M.
Can you use WordPerfect, word processing? Yes_____ NO_____

Millikin University

The library hires students to work in several different areas. Please read the following brief descriptions and rank the jobs in order of preference (1 would be most interest). If a job is not open in your preferred area, you may be considered for one of the other jobs. The number of hours per week may be affected by Work/Study constraints.

Acquisitions:
The Acquisitions student searches for books using the computer, types cards, and takes the mail to the mailroom in Shilling Hall.

5 hours a week - 1 hour a day in the afternoon around 3:30 p.m.

Circulation:
Circulation students assist patrons, answer the phone, maintain machines, shelve, circulate materials, do some computer searching, and do some light typing.

8 - 10 hours a week (maybe more if desired) - Some day & evening hours (possibly until 11 p.m.) and every other weekend.

Interlibrary Loan:
ILL students retrieve books and periodicals to be loaned out. They also photocopy articles, type periodical requests, search for items on the computer, and label items to be sent out.

10 hours a week - 2 hours each day during the day.

Periodicals:
Periodical students shelve, straighten and maintain the periodicals. They also assist with special periodical projects such as binding and inventory.

10 hours a week - hours can be flexible, some weekends hours are desired.

Reference:
Reference student helps grade papers and update assignments using WordPerfect.

8 hours a week.

Technical Services:
Technical Services assistant files, checks shelves, and does some computer searching.

5 hours a week - may be combined with Acquisitions position.

Rank:
_____Acquisitions   _____Circulation _____Interlibrary Loan
_____Periodicals   _____Reference   _____Technical Services

MYRIN LIBRARY
STUDENT ASSISTANT APPLICATION FORM

Ursinus College

Name:_____   Campus Phone:_____
        (Last)   (First)

Campus Address:_____

Home Address:_____
         (Street)   (City/State)   (Zip Code)

Class:_____   Social Security Number:_____
   (List Year)

Major/Minor:_____

Extracurricular Activities (please check):

_____Clubs, Name_____

_____Volunteer Work, Name_____

_____Sports, Name_____

_____Other, Name_____

Hobbies:_____

Have you been offered work study as part of your financial aid
package?_____

Do you have any library work experience? _____ If yes, what
did you do? _____

Do you presently work on campus?_____   If yes, where?

_____

Previous work experience: _____

_____

_____

How many hours a week are you available to work? (minimun of 5/wk)

_____

Are you able to work during: _____ Evenings?

_____ Weekends?   _____ Christmas Vacation?

_____ Long Weekends?

Ursinus College

Would you be interested in working during the summer? _____

Skills (Please check appropriate items):

_____Typing (WPM:_____)   _____AV Equipment

_____Computer Work   _____Filing

_____Artistic   _____General Office Work

_____Languages (Name:_____)

_____Other (Specify:_____)

Do you prefer to work:

_____At a service desk   _____In a processing area

_____In Media Services (AV)   _____No preference

You may provide any additional information below that we may find helpful in processing this application.

Signature:_____ Date:_____

FOR LIBRARY USE ONLY

Comments:

This student has been hired in _____
                                        (Department)

by _____. Date: _____
      (Supervisor)

66 - Employment/Dismissal

University of Wisconsin - Superior

APPLICATION FOR EMPLOYMENT
JIM DAN HILL LIBRARY
UNIVERSITY OF WISCONSIN-SUPERIOR

NAME _____ SS#_____

LOCAL ADDRESS _____ TELEPHONE NUMBER _____

PERMANENT ADDRESS _____ TELEPHONE NUMBER _____

_____

WORK STUDY _____ STUDENT ASSISTANT _____

YEAR IN SCHOOL _____ MAJOR _____ MINOR _____

HOURS AVAILABLE FOR WORK:

Mon _____ Tues _____ Wed _____ Thurs _____ Fri _____

CAN YOU WORK: Evenings until 10:00 p.m. _____ Weekends _____

When would you be available to begin work _____

DURING THE ACADEMIC SCHOOL YEAR WOULD YOU PREFER TO WORK:

Less than 10 hrs/week _____ 10-14 hrs/week _____ 15-20 hrs/week _____

Would you be available to work during break periods _____

SKILLS:

Typing _____   Art Work _____   COMPUTERS
Filing _____   Book Mending _____   Inputting _____
Word Processing _____ Office Machines _____   Programming _____
                        Specify _____   Courses _____
                        _____

Do you prefer a job where you: (Please check one)
  work with the public _____   do not have to deal with the public _____
  are involved with the public some of the time _____

PREVIOUS JOB EXPERIENCE

Please give a brief description of previous jobs you have held. Note any
library experience (shelving, processing, searching) you have had.

Name and address of most recent employer _____

Supervisor's Name _____ Telephone No. _____

Employment/Dismissal - 67

The College of Wooster

REFERENCE REPLY FORM:

Reference Contact's Name _____
        office phone no.   _____
        home phone no.   _____

Reference Check for: _____

1.   Relationship betwee reference contact and student:
        _____advisor
        _____professor
        _____employer
        _____other

2.   How long have you know this student? _____

3.   What types of work did this student do for you?
        _____class work
        _____assistantship
        _____other_____

4.   Would this person be punctual and reliable?
        _____yes
        _____no

5.   Would this person be thorough and concise, and pay close attention to detail work?
        _____yes
        _____no

6.   Would this person be trustworthy?
        _____yes
        _____no

7.   Was this person ever a discipline problem?
        _____yes
        _____no

8.   How well does this student work with other students? (loner? team player?...)

9.   Is there anything else good or bad that we should know about this person?

10.   Summary of reference contact's opinion of this person:

Indiana Wesleyan University

Goodman Library
Indiana Wesleyan University
Recommendation Form

Candidate's Name _____ Date:_____

The Person whose name appears above has requested employment with us.
He/she has given us your name to contact. Please rate this person as
best as you can. If you feel impressed to telephone us, please do so
or request that we call you and in that case, please provide your
telephone number.

1.   Length of time you have known this person: _____
2.   Type of work done for you or your company:_____
     _____
3.   Personal appearance: Well groomed___Acceptable___
     Poorly groomed___
4.   Work attendance: Excellent___Fair___Poor___
5.   Punctuality and dependability: Always___Usually___Seldom___
6.   Job performance: Excellent___Very good___Average___Fair___Poor___
7.   Speech: Fluent___Fair___Poor___
8.   Gets along with others: Very well___Moderately well___Poorly___
9.   Would you rehire if opportunity arose?_ _____
10. Any further comment or message you might like to give us:_____
     _____
     _____
11. Personality: (please comment briefly) _____
12. Cooperativeness: Excellent___ Good ___ Poor ___
13. Creativeness: Excellent___ Good ___ Poor ___

     Date_____Signature _____Phone no._____
       Please return this form to: Director, Goodman Library 4201 S.
     Washington St. Marion, IN   46953 Phone No.: 317-677-2334

==
I hereby authorize the Goodman Library to investigate my past
employment and all facts stated in my information form. I also assume
that Goodman Library will contact persons I have given for personal
references. I release from all liability or responsibility all
persons, places of business, or governmental agencies regarding
information provided on this form.

_____   _____
        DATE   APPLICANT SIGNATURE

Ripon College

RiponCollegeLibrary
Student Assistant Work Interview Form

Name: Date:

Current campus address: Phone:

Current class status: Freshmen   Sophomore   Junior   Senior

Request for school year employment: Term_____   Year_____

Summer_____

Major: GPA:

Library Experience:

Campus Experience:

Other Experience:

Have you ever been fired from a job? (If yes, explain)

Why do you want to work in the library?

What are your extra curricular activities?

Could you work nights or weekends?

Where is your home town?

Is there anything you would like to tell us about yourself that we haven't asked?

Interviewer's comments:

70 - Employment/Dismissal

Lebanon Valley College
of Pennsylvania

STUDENT CONTRACT

1. Students are to report "5" minutes before their scheduled hour, and leave "5" minutes before the hour (or half hour). Within minutes of arrival check with Mrs. K for task assignment. In her absence you are expected to report to the workroom for assignment. Other staff personnel will require your services. When you have completed each task report back to supervisor(s). You are accountable to ALL staff members. You are expected to use your time here in an ethical manner. When you work desk and your replacement is late, you need not stay -But DO make sure you have notified staff the desk is unmanned.

2. Personal visiting is to be kept in line with the workload. When there is work - please keep visiting to a minimum. When we hit a peak workload please make arrangements to visit later. Keep a low profile behind the desk (not party time). Do not allow patrons behind the desk.

3. The Student Library Assistant position is more demanding than in previous times as more services are made available within the library. Your grades will suffer if you PLAN ON DESK DUTY AS STUDY TIME, but you are encouraged to bring study/reading material "SHOULD" work-load time allow for it.

4. Finals Week - You are expected to work Finals Week between 5 and 8 hours. Those who have a "good work attitude" will receive more consideration in this and all scheduling/time off.

ABSENCES

1. YOU ARE RESPONSIBLE FOR ALL ASSIGNED HOURS. If you are unable to be here for ANY reason, notify Mrs. K (or Mrs. M.). We expect a phone call from you personally (except in cases of extreme illness). You are expected to find replacements for all evening (any hours after 4:00) and weekend hours. Replacements for WEEKDAY "daytime" slots are "not always" necessary, BUT it is YOUR responsibility to check with Mrs. K (or Mrs. M.) concerning this.

REPLACEMENTS - Please take your work slots seriously!!!!!

USE THE BULLETIN BOARD TO POST YOUR REPLACEMENT NEEDS, LET MRS. K KNOW ABOUT ALL CHANGES. YOU WILL BE GIVEN A LIST OF ALL STUDENT WORKERS/PHONE #'s. Keep it handy. The list is also posted on the board.

FAILURE TO REPORT FOR WORK

    1ST UNEXCUSED ABSENCE - WARNING

    2ND UNEXCUSED ABSENCE - WARNING + LETTER TO DIRECTOR

    3RD UNEXCUSED ABSENCE - TERMINATION

HAVING READ THE POLICY MANUAL, DRUG FREE WORKPLACE POLICY, AND THIS CONTRACT I AGREE TO ACCEPT AND FOLLOW ALL RULES AND PROCEDURES.

SIGNATURE_____ DATE_____

Linfield College

CIRCULATION STUDENT-WORKER CONTRACT

The primary goal of Northup Library is to be actively involved in the teaching/learning process of the college. It is the primary responsibility of the library staff and Circulation Student Worker to support this goal by working together to develop and maintain a program of quality service to the academic community.

The following are requirements for the position of Circulation Student Worker:

1. Circulation students represent the library and are expected to be courteous and helpful to all library patrons. Circulation students should be neat and clean in appearance and dressed in appropriate work attire.

2. Circulation students are responsible for learning, consistently following and enforcing established Library policies and procedures.

3. Circulation students are to remain alert and attentive, doing assigned work accurately. Eating in the library is not acceptable. Studying is allowed only in special circumstances.

4. Circulation students are responsible for the security and care of library materials, equipment, and supplies. Library supplies are for official library use only.

5. Circulation students must report to work promptly and work their fully assigned shift. Absences are permitted only in cases of illness or personal emergency. Plan your time so that you are prepared for tests or papers due without needing time off from work. In case of illness or personal emergency please notify the Circulation Supervisor as soon as possible. It is the responsibility of the circulation student to find a substitute. Circulation students who are absent without notification and without finding a substitute may be dropped from Library employment.

An evaluation will take place during the middle of each semester of work and a discussion between student and supervisor will follow. If the supervisor feels that a student needs improvement in a certain area, s/he will discuss the specific problem with the student and a reasonable time for improvement will be set. If there has not been adequate improvement after this period of time, the student may be dismissed from the employment of the library. An end of the semester evaluation will also take place, and will include a recommendation for continued employment within the library if appropriate.

       I have read and understand the above requirements for this position. I understand that failure to   fulfill these requirements may result in termination.

_____   _____
Student Worker's signature   Date

_____   _____
Supervisor's signature   Date

Lorette Wilmot Library

TO: READER SERVICES STUDENT WORKERS
FR: LINDA WILLIAMS, MAIN DESK SUPERVISOR
RE: STUDENT ASSISTANT POLICIES

Welcome to the Lorette Wilmot Library as a student assistant. Please read and sign this policy sheet in order that we both understand what the general expectations are for student workers in the Reader Services department. The directions that you receive from your immediate supervisor will supersede these instructions. If you have any questions, please ask a supervisor.

1. Absence without notification or consistent tardiness are grounds for dismissal. If you are unable to work your shift, you are expected to find a replacement and to notify your supervisor of your absence, as soon as possible. If your shift becomes inconvenient for any reason, please let us know so that we may attempt to adjust it.

2. Your appearance and attitude at work are most important. Your demeanor at any desk or in any department should be respectful and professional. Your attire should be appropriate and include shoes. If you have any questions about what is appropriate dress, please ask.

3. The only time that you are not expected to be in the library, and on time, for your shift is during those periods in which the dormitories are closed. This means that during social events you are expected to fulfill your employment obligations to the library, either through working or arranging for a substitute to work for you.

4. Breaks are to be for fifteen minutes for every four hour slot that you work. You may not take your break during the first or the last fifteen minutes of your work shift. Breaks must always be cleared with your supervisor.

5. When you are assigned to the Main Desk your primary responsibility is the coverage of that desk. The Main Desk is under no circumstances to be left unattended. You will, however, be expected to perform other duties, such as re-shelving returned books and reading the shelves when the Main Desk coverage is adequate. One further note – it would be difficult to overestimate the importance of your work in re-shelving and shelf reading; if the material is not exactly where it should be, then it is worthless.

6. Your work time, whether at the desk or in the stacks, is not to be used primarily for socializing. Patrons always take precedence over personal conversations and homework. You may not invite associates behind the desk – library staff only.

7. Work time can be used for study only after you have completed your duties at the desk. Please do not fill up counter space with notebooks and papers. You are not allowed to use typewriters and other machines for your personal use.

8. Supplies available for patrons are in the supply box at the desk. You are not welcome to go into supervisors' desks for additional supplies.

9. Remember, you are not a Reference Librarian. You are not expected to answer questions such as strategies for locating articles on child abuse. You are expected to supply general information such as library hours and location of photocopy machines. Please remember not to send patrons away without an answer. If a Reference Librarian is not available, refer the patron to your supervisor. If your supervisor is not available, make sure you take a message with a telephone number, so that someone can get back to the patron.

10. One last note: student assistants are hired for one semester at a time -- no one is automatically rehired. You can also be dismissed during the semester if it is found that you cannot follow our policies.

_____   _____
Student Signature   Date

Southern Utah University

EMPLOYMENT CONTRACT

I, _____ understand that as one of the requirements of acceptance of a job in the library, I am required to take IM101 <u>Library Orientation</u> during my first quarter of employment and receive a grade of a B- or better.

There will be four options for students who are employed at the library.

1. **Take class for credit.** Must receive a grade of B- or above.
2. **Register for audit.** Complete five worksheets and take the final test. Must receive a grade of B- or above.
3. **Library Training.** Do not register. Attend classes and complete all worksheets and take the final test. Must receive a grade of B- or above.
4. **Take the final test** of IM101 during the first quarter of employment and receive a grade of 82% or above.

I understand that I am expected to enforce all library rules and regulations and maintain the privacy of the library user. There are **NO** exceptions. To do so would be breaking the law and I understand I will be held liable for any breaches of this library security.

_____
Signature of worker

_____
Date

_____
Signature of Supervisor

NOTE: The clothes you wear to work should reflect your desire to continue your employment.

Southwest Baptist University

Southwest Baptist University

BOLIVAR, MISSOURI 65613-2496 • (417) 326-5281

<u>ESTEP LIBRARY WORK-STUDY AGREEMENT</u>

_____, .I.D. # _____ is
assigned to work in the _____ area. The supervisor of
this area is _____. Student workers are
expected to follow the directions given by their supervisor, other
library staff, or librarians. Student workers must learn, and will
be held responsible, for knowing the procedures and rules in the
department to which they are assigned. This information will be
provided to you.

In addition to the specific daily assignments provided by your
supervisor, you <u>MUST</u>:
    -know when you are scheduled to work and be on time;
    -contact your supervisor if you cannot work and arrange for
        another worker, if a circulation desk worker, to work
        your scheduled time;
    -dress <u>appropriately</u> to greet the public;
    -carefully and thoroughly complete all tasks assigned to you;
    -report any problems to your supervisor;
    -sign in/out each time you work and keep track of your hours
        being careful not to go over your allowed total;
    -conduct yourself in a manner appropriate as a representative
        of both the library and the university;
    request another assignment when your regular assignment is
        done.

AS A STUDENT WORKER YOU <u>SHOULD NOT</u>:
    -waste time, socialize, use the library phone (except in case
        of library business or emergency), or study while on
        library time;
    -make any distinction or show any favoritism among library
        patrons;
    -disclose <u>any information about any library patron</u> to other
        individuals.

If you agree to abide by this contract, please sign both copies of
this. Give one copy to your supervisor and one to Dr. VanBlair's
secretary.

_____   _____
Student Worker   Date

Transylvania University

Circulation Department
Transylvania University Library

EMPLOYMENT AGREEMENT

Employee Name: _____ Date: _____

Schedule for _____(term)   _____(year)

The library agrees to employ you through the coming term provided that the requirements listed below are met.

The schedule below is for the entire term. If you need to make changes see Mrs. Mary Ruth Clark.

Attendance: Failure to report for your scheduled work time will result in both a verbal and written warning. A copy of the Dismissal Warning will be sent to the Financial Aid office. A further occurrence will result in termination from the library.

Substitutes for planned absences (including T. U. sponsored events): You may have another library worker substitute for you if you have filled out a Student Substitute Form. This must be signed by you, the substitute and a staff member.

Illness: We expect you to locate a substitute using the Student Staff Directory as distributed. If you are not able to locate a substitute after making a serious effort or in case of a grave emergency, call Mrs. Clark or George Campbell on duty and advise them of your difficulty.

Your schedule:

Monday: _____

Tuesday: _____

Wednesday: _____

Thursday: _____

Friday: _____

Saturday: _____

Sunday: _____

76 - Employment/Dismissal

I understand and accept the following responsibilities:

- to work the above scheduled hours for the entire term.

- to work equivalent hours (to be arranged) during the Exam period.

- to arrive promptly for scheduled work hours and to notify supervisor if unavoidably detained.

- to arrange for a substitute (according to stated procedures) or notify your supervisor in case of grave emergencies.

- to become familiar with the Circulation Desk Manual.

- to master in a reasonable time the requirements of my assignment.

- failure to report for scheduled work hours will result in my dismissal.

Signed: _____

Date: _____

Luther College

DISCIPLINARY ACTION NOTICE

NAME _____   SPO _____   DATE _____

PRNO # _____   DEPT. _____

____   1st Warning   As a result of this violation, you are being
                           reprimanded for your actions.

____   2nd Warning   This is a second reprimand. Should a third
                           be required, your student work allocation
                           will be terminated.

____   TERMINATION   The Personnel Office has received notification
                           from this department that your student work
                           has been terminated as of _____.
                           In accordance with your agreement with this
                           department and the Personnel Office your
                           student work allocation is terminated. If
                           you are working an additional job this will
                           not be affected but you will not be able to
                           transfer your student work hours from this
                           department to another.

Date of Violation _____

Explanation and Remarks:

Copies to: Supervisor's Signature

1. Student   _____
2. Office Personnel Services   Date: _____
 78 - Employment/Dismissal

Even though the handbook has tried to clearly state its expectations occasionally the behavior of a student aide will require his/her Manager to refer to the following statement on "Grounds for Dismissal". It is your responsibility to be aware of these dismissal conditions and procedures. If you have any questions, please direct them to your supervisor.

A. You as a student aide may be dismissed for any of the following reasons:

1. Refusal to do assigned tasks.

2. Frequent tardiness or absenteeism.

3. Unauthorized use of library materials, facilities or supplies.

4. Improper reporting of hours in a time card.

5. Consistently poor job performance or inadequate job skills.

6. Failure to maintain a positive service-minded approach toward patrons, staff or co-workers.

7. Reporting to work under the influence of alcohol or a controlled substance.

8. Insubordination.

B. In case of failure to meet the library's expectations as evidenced by one or more of the above reasons, these procedures generally will be followed by your Manager:

1. Verbal warning

2. Written warning

3. Dismissal

The Manager may bypass step one and proceed immediately to step two if circumstances warrant. The student is not eligible for a transfer to another department until such time as he/she shows the Manager satisfactory improvement concerning the conduct in question. In addition, the student will not receive any more warnings after step two prior to employment termination.
The Library Director maintains the right to terminate immediately the employment of a student assistant for serious violations of A. 1 through A. 8 above.

C. If your overall job performance is determined to be marginal, and if after sufficient warning there is no significant improvement, you will not be rehired for a subsequent academic term.

Springfield College

STUDENT EMPLOYEE REMINDER SLIP

BABSON LIBRARY - SPRINGFIELD COLLEGE

Dear_____,

THIS IS NOT A WARNING

  This is to make you aware of a situation in which you did not correctly follow library and/or student employee policy:

_____

_____

_____

_____

  Please make an effort to not allow this to happen again. Please be advised that repetition of the above infringement will result in a warning slip.

  If you have questions about this reminder, please ask. We want to help you correct this situation.

Circulation Supr's Sig_____Date_____

Issued By_____Date_____

  Additional comments may be placed below.

STUDENT EMPLOYEE WARNING SLIP
BABSON LIBRARY
SPRINGFIELD COLLEGE

Dear_____,

    Please be advised of this warning in regards to your:

_____

_____

_____

_____

    We encourage you to put forth every effort to amend the above inappropriate work behavior or termination of your position as student employee at Babson Library will be effective immediately!

    You have the right to appeal the above action.

Circulation Supr's Sig_____Date_____

Warning Issued By_____Date_____

    Additional comments may be placed below.

ORIENTATION AND TRAINING

Elmira College
IV. WHO DOES WHAT.

A. The Director. The Director oversees all operations and all GTL Departments in the building. His immediate superior is the Academic Dean. If a Student Worker is unsure about to whom a question should be referred, it may be referred to the Director.

B. Public Services. Public Services in the GTL oversees Circulation and Periodicals. It includes the following personnel and functions:

1. Public Services Librarian. The Public Services Librarian reports to the Library Director. At the present time the Public Services Librarian is in charge of Circulation, Periodicals, the College Archives and the Mark Twain Archives. Any questions relative to these areas may be referred to him.

2. Circulation Manager. The Circulation Manager reports to the Public Services Librarian and is in charge of all Circulation functions. Questions concerning Circulation matters, such as fines, overdue books etc. should be referred to her. In addition, the Circulation manager takes care of the copiers and card machines and should be made aware of any problems with these.

The Circulation manager directly supervises the Student workers in Circulation and is the person to whom any problems of scheduling etc. should be referred.

3. Circulation Assistant. The Circulation Assistant works half-time in Circulation and half-time as Processing-Assistant. As Circulation Assistant she reports to the Circulation Manager and is responsible for Circulation functions including Overdue notices and Reserves. In the absence of the Circulation Manager questions may be referred to the Circulation Assistant.

4. Periodicals Specialist. The Periodicals Specialist reports to the Public Services Librarian and is responsible for maintaining the periodicals collection. This includes checking in periodicals and maintaining the current and back issues shelves, the newspapers and the GTL holdings list. Any questions regarding our periodical holdings (missing issues etc.) may be referred to her.

C. Technical Services. Technical Services is the area responsible for ordering, cataloging and processing books and other library materials. They maintain the card catalog and use the OCLC system for cataloging and Inter-Library Loan.

1. Technical Services Librarian. The Technical Services Librarian reports to the Library Director. At this time the Technical Services Librarian is in charge of Cataloging, Bookkeeping/Acquisitions and Inter-Library Loan.

2. Cataloging Specialist. The Cataloging Specialist reports to the Technical Services Librarian and is responsible for cataloging new acquisitions, processing and repairing books and maintaining the card catalog.

3. Acquisitions Specialist. The Acquisitions Specialist reports to the Technical Services Librarian and is in charge of ordering books, supplies and equipment and in keeping the financial records of the GTL.

4. Cataloging Assistant. The Cataloging Assistant works half-time as Circulation-Assistant. As Cataloging Assistant she reports to the Technical Services Librarian and is responsible for readying newly acquired materials for Circulation as well as other Technical Services tasks as requested.

5. ILL Specialist. The Inter-Library Loan Specialist reports to the Technical Services Librarian and is responsible for filling ILL requests that we receive from our students and from other libraries. In her absence, questions may be referred to the Technical Services Librarian.

D.Reference. The Reference Department oversees Reference service, including database searching and library instruction. At this time, the Government Documents Collection is also maintained by the Reference Department.

1. Reference Librarian. The Reference Librarian reports to the Library Director. She is in charge of the Reference Collection, including ordering of Reference books, CD services, On-Line searching and Library Instruction. She is also in charge of Government Documents.

2. Documents Assistant. The Documents Assistant is in charge of maintaining the Government Documents Collection. Any questions regarding Documents may be referred to her.

Elmira College

E. Media. The Media office is in charge of all non-book materials such as film, audio tape, video tape etc. and also for equipment such as VCR's, tape players, projectors and microphones.

1. Media Office Manager. The Media Office Manager reports to the Library Director and is responsible for ordering of audio-visual materials, reserving all rooms in the GTL - including 04, 06 and other classrooms - and for overseeing the general operations of the Media Office.

2. Audio-Visual Manager. The Audio-Visual Manager reports to the Library Director and is responsible for scheduling, maintaining and setting-up AV equipment campus wide and for overseeing the general operations of the Media Office.

3. Photographer/Graphic Artist. The Photographer/Graphic Artist reports to the Library Director and is responsible for photography and special projects involving Graphic design, for maintaining the photo area and darkrooms and teaches photography classes. At this time she is also advisor to the Yearbook.

4. Media Office Receptionist. The Media Office Receptionist reports to the Media Office Manager and is responsible for answering the phone and maintaining the Media collection as requested.

5. Audio-Visual Technician. The Audio-Visual Technician reports to the Audio-Visual Manager and is responsible for maintaining the AV equipment and performing equipment set-ups as requested.

FOLKE
BERNADOTTE
MEMORIAL LIBRARY

STUDENT ORIENTATION GUIDELINES

These guidelines have been prepared to help you, the library student assistant, understand what is expected of you as an employee of the Folke Bernadotte Memorial Library and the Lund Music-Speech Library.

The following policies and guidelines are to be followed by all library student assistants, regardless of where you work in the library. However, each supervisor will have his/her own set of expectations based on the activities and responsibilities of the particular department. It is your responsibility to be certain you understand and are aware of these.

WORK SCHEDULES

You should report to the library as soon as possible in the first week of classes each term. You and your supervisor will then determine how the hours assigned to you by the Financial Aid Office are to be spent throughout the academic year.

Your position as a student assistant will require learning many things in a short time. Your immediate supervisor will arrange for your training in the certain tasks or activities you will be required to perform. It is important that you attend meetings and ask questions when you are in doubt or when you do not know. This is the way to learn and to avoid making errors.

PAYROLL REPORTING

You will record your work hours on the computer time clock located in the Circulation Services Department. A computer generated payroll card is kept by your immediate supervisor in your assigned work area. To receive a paycheck, you must sign the timecard no later than the 3rd of each month. Students working during the academic year are paid on the 15th of each month.

Student assistants working four consecutive hours are entitled to a 15-minute paid break. Students working full days when classes are not in session must clock out for a 30-minute lunch break. These students are also entitled to two 15-minute paid breaks—one in the morning and one in the afternoon.

Gustavus Adolphus College

ATTENDANCE

You are expected to report for work according to the work schedule you and your supervisor have planned together, unless you have made <u>previous</u> arrangements with your supervisor.

When you are unable to work due to a sickness or an emergency, it is <u>your</u> responsibility to let your supervisor know as soon as possible.

An unexcused absence will result in both a verbal and written dismissal warning. A copy of the completed form will be sent to the Financial Aid Office. The second occurrence will result in termination of library employment. It could also lead to loss of your work/study award. Scheduled work hours occur during Christmas in Christ Chapel; Greek Rush; and all break periods when school is in session—Nobel, May Day, Fall Break, and Reading Days. Regular work schedules should be followed unless you have made prior arrangements with your supervisor.

WORK RESPONSIBILITIES AND EVALUATION

You will receive training and assignments from your immediate supervisor. Each spring you will be evaluated by your supervisor for performance review and retention purposes.

DRESS & CONDUCT

Although there is not a rigid dress code for working in the library, you are expected to dress appropriately. Shoes must be worn. Halter tops or swimsuits, for example, are not considered suitable. No Greek initiation clothing should be worn during your shift. Use of headphones at a public service desk are not acceptable.

The library atmosphere should be conducive to research and work. Please do your part by avoiding extended or loud conversations with your friends or fellow workers which interfere with your library duties and with the work of library users.

TELEPHONES

Personal calls should not be made on telephones in the library, nor should you receive personal calls unless it is an emergency. A telephone located outside the entrance of the library may be used without charge for personal calls during non-work hours.

Staff members will answer the telephones as often as possible, but you should not hesitate to do so when a staff member is not available or when you see a staff member is busy.

TRANSYLVANIA UNIVERSITY LIBRARY
STUDENT ASSISTANT ORIENTATION

Student's Name _____ Date _____

Supervisor _____

Shift/Hour One

The Essentials

_____   Time clock procedure

_____   Work study time sheet

_____   Contracts (replacements, warning form, etc.)

_____   Evaluation

_____   Eating, smoking, drinking

_____   Dress code

_____   Basic tour of library - main floor (restrooms, water fountains, vending machines, lounge)

_____   Basic responsibilities

_____   Assignment

_____   Schedule

Shift/Hour Two

The Workplace

_____   Work schedule

_____   Pick up signed contracts

_____   Introduction to library staff

_____   More extensive tour of the library

_____   Personal articles - don't leave book bags laying around

Transylvania University

Student Assistants

_____ Layout of the circulation desk area – where everything is

- Security systems (2)

- Reserves

- Holding shelves (ILL, miscell., Lost & Found)

- Safe areas for holding A-V equipment
- Pre-shelving areas for books, current & back periodicals

- Search request cards

- ILL forms

- Miscellaneous forms in black box (Reserve Request forms, maps, etc.)

Telephone

_____ How to answer (role playing)

_____ Message taking (3 messages to be critiqued by supervisor)

_____ Sound of another call coming in

_____ Public telephones

_____ Personal phone calls (not allowed)

Cash drawer

_____ Copy monies

_____ Fine monies

_____ IOU's (none allowed)

_____ Vending machine refunds

Copy machines

_____ Use of binders/accurate record-keeping (Old students need to record old (first) number

_____ Problems (notify MRC or George)

_____ Paper

_____ "Bad" copies (3 only allowed)

_____ Adding paper

_____ Notify Mary Ruth when paper is low

_____ Toner needed (notify MRC or George)

_____ Read Introduction & Student Responsibilities section in the Circulation Manual, as well as p. 17 and the Location Section.

90 - Orientation and Training

Student Assistants

Hour/Shift Three

Online Training

_____   General overview & manipulation of terminal and light pen

_____   Logging-on/off (password)

_____   Updating of patron record (use Harlan Sanders)

_____   Registration of new patron (register self)

_____   Checking out a book

_____   Reference books (example of book not checked out)

_____   Different due dates

_____   Different types of patrons

_____   Audio-visual materials

_____   Desensitize books

_____   New date due slip - write date when first glued in

_____   Limits

_____   Blocks - refer to p. 18 of Circulation Manual

Reserves

_____   Location

_____   Different types

_____   Two at a time

_____   When B,C, & D reserves can be taken out

_____   DO NOT de-sensitize

_____   What to say to patron when reserves taken out; reminder (date/time due slip) put in B, C & D reserves material

_____   Read p. 7-10, 13-14 of the Circulation Manual.

Transylvania University

Student Assistants

Shift/Day Four

Checking-In Materials

_____   Overstamping & initialing

_____   Re-sensitizing

_____   Remove paper clips, pieces of paper

_____   Need repair?

_____   Placing books on shelf

_____   Shelving Thomas/oversize/Ref

_____   Educational Resources Center

_____   Overdues and fines

Reserves

_____   Check-in immediately

_____   Shelve immediately

_____   Do LC Easy

_____   Read p. 11-12 of the Circulation Manual.

Shift/Hour Five

Periodicals

_____   Do not check out (see supervisor)

_____   Shelving current - each shift

_____   Keeping in order (back issues)

_____   Go through Miscellaneous Section of the Circulation Manual, p. 19-23. (Go through this with student, using Manual as checklist.)

Transalyvania University

Student Assistants

Additional Information

_____   Emergency (Discuss procedure as noted on the Circulation Manual cover)

_____   Audio-visual/conference room requests

_____   ProQuest (Train student only in basics and how to put paper in printer; refer anything else to full-time staff.)

_____   Review Circulation Manual (note Index)

_____   Review of staff and positions

_____   Studying (a privilege - don't put off studying to do it here)

_____   Shelf-reading assignment (take student to area)

_____   See Murder in the Stacks

_____   Informational/reference questions

_____   Procedures Manual for Weekend Duty

Haverford College

CARE AND HANDLING OF LIBRARY MATERIALS

The College maintains libraries in order to make accessible to the campus community materials that individual students and faculty could not practically own for personal use. Since library materials are communal resources, everyone in the College is responsible for taking care of them; to discharge this responsibility successfully and protect this vital communal investment, library users will have to be, in many cases, more careful with library materials than they might be with items in their personal library.

Careful handling of library materials does a great deal to increase their life expectancy and usefulness, and each of us can contribute to protecting the College's library collections by adopting some simple practices for handling them. In working with library materials, therefore, please observe the following:

1. Food and drink can cause both immediate and indirect damage to library materials. Spilled beverages, food particles, and greasy fingers can leave stains or unsightly garbage on materials; furthermore, food wrappers and traces of food, even food that has been properly disposed of in wastebaskets, can attract such vermin as silverfish, roaches, and mice that will happily feed on paper, book glues, etc. after they have finished with the food leavings.

    a. Do not eat while working with library materials.
    b. Wash your hands before handling library materials.
    c. Eat and drink only in the staff lounge, never in the stacks or reading areas.
    d. If you see people eating in the library, explain our concern to them and ask them to snack outside the building.

2. Dust accumulated on library materials can act as a sponge for moisture and become a breeding ground for mold that will attack paper. Keep library materials dust free.

3. Books are relatively fragile; they survive longer if they are gently handled and are not called upon to sustain repeated shocks.

    a. Do not stack books in large piles that are likely to fall over.
    b. Store books flat or upright.
    c. Books on a shelf should be firmly but not too tightly supported in their full upright position.
    d. Do not let books lean on a shelf; leaning puts uncomfortable pressure on the spine.
    e. If a book is too tall for the shelf, lower the shelf or shelve the book on its spine, not its foredge, because shelving a book on its foredge weakens the spine.
    f. When taking a book off the shelf, especially if the book is tightly wedged on the shelf, do not pull it off the shelf by grabbing its cap; rather, loosen the books on the shelf, put your hand around the spine of the book, and apply pressure to the covers.
    g. When reading a book, especially if it is new, open it gently; do not bend back the covers; do not leave a book open "face down" on a table.
    h. Turn pages gently to decrease danger of tearing them, and never crease a page to mark your place.
    i. Do not apply pressure to library materials when photocopying them.
    j. Do not use rubber bands, post-it notes, pressure-sensitive tapes, or paperclips on library materials because they can mutilate pages.

k. Use a single piece of paper as a bookmark; do not try to close a book if several several sheets of paper are inserted in it.

4. Never write in or otherwise mark library materials. When taking notes, use a pencil so if you accidentally mark the book or journal you can erase the mark.

5. Do not let library materials get wet.

6. Do not expose library materials to high heat or store them in direct sunlight.

9/1/93
RHK

Sweet Briar College

Care for the Library's Collections

—Handle all library materials with clean hands. Make sure workspaces and work surfaces are clean. Fingerprints, and food or beverage stains can be indelible.

—Do not wedge or pack books tightly on a shelf. Make sure that materials can be retrieved easily, without causing damage.

—If you find books tightly wedged together, do not tug on a book to remove it from the shelf. First, move the bookend over to loosen the pressure on the books. Then remove your book.

-- Handle microfilm and microfiche by the edges, as you would a photograph. Smudges and scratches obliterate microformat images.

--Compact discs, laser discs and phonograph records should be held by the edges. Fingerprints can cause chemical damage in plastics.

--Never desensitize videotapes, audiocassettes or computer diskettes! Desensitizing will erase these media.

—Do not attach metal paper clips to book pages for any reason, as they crimp or tear paper, and can leave rust stains.

—Do not turn down the corners of pages. Creases become permanent and weaken the paper.

—Laying an open book face down will damage the binding.

—When photocopying books, take care not to wrinkle pages. Do not force a book flat to copy it as this can damage the binding.

—Bring damaged materials to the attention of Mrs. Reid or Ms. Johnston. **Do not attempt to make repairs yourself**, as many glues and tapes will further damage books.

Greenville College

NAME: _____

	FIRST SEMESTER	OCT. REVIEW	SECOND SEMESTER	APRIL REVIEW	COMMENTS
QUICK REFERENCE PAGE					
LIBRARY TOUR					
CHECKING OUT — IN					
BOOKS					
LCLS BOOKS					
MAGAZINES					
PAMPHLETS					
RESERVES					
TESTS					
RENEWING MATERIALS					
CHARGING OVERDUES					
ATTENDANCE COUNTS					
INITIALING					
TIME CARDS					
SHELVES — DAILY					
SHELF — READING					
SHELVING BOOKS, ETC.					
RESHELVING					
RESHELVING MAGAZINES					
PHOTOCOPIES					
TYPEWRITER					
ALARM SYSTEMS					
FIRE ALARMS					
DOOR ALARMS					
BOOK ALARMS					
PHONE CALLS					
GUEST CARDS					
TEST FILES					
CLOSING					

TELEPHONE — SERVICE

May I Take a Message?

Have you ever gotten a slip of paper from someone in the office noting that you received a phone call from someone whose name you don't recognize? You rack your brains trying to figure out who it can be. A client? A supplier? A secret admirer?

Even though cryptic messages provide moments of intrigue in an otherwise humdrum existence, businesses don't run very efficiently on them.

The more information you get from callers, the better. Whenever you must answer a call for someone, always try to get the following information and write it down:

1) Date and time of call.
2) Complete name, including title: *Mr. Lesley Nielsen, Ms. Dana Hunter.*
3) Organization and nature of call: *Southern Telephone Co., re: broken phone. Service call needs to be rescheduled.*
4) Instructions or action to be taken: *Please return call by noon today.*
5) Phone number of caller, including area code, if necessary.
6) Your name or initials in case the person for whom you took the message has any questions.

When in doubt about what to write down, just imagine that the call was for you, and it *was* that secret admirer. What kind of information would you want in the message? ◨

PROFESSIONAL TIPS TO INSURE EFFECTIVE HANDLING OF INCOMING CALLS

1) The telephone is <u>not</u> an interruption. It is an important part of customer service.

2) Answer the telephone in a pleasant, distinctive voice.

3) Always get the caller's name.

4) Concentrate on what the caller is saying and repeat the information back.

5) Never tell a caller, "No, " "He/She is on break," or "He/She is at lunch." Instead offer a positive alternative like, "He/She is not available right now. May I take a message?"

6) Never say "I don't know." Instead say, "I'll find out for you." or "I can refer you to someone who can answer that."

7) Instead of saying "I can't."; offer an alternative like, "Let's try this..." or "Let's see what we can do."

8) Never tell callers to "hold on" before putting them on hold or transferring the call. Instead ask, "Are you able to hold?"

9) Never tell a caller "You'll have to..." Instead say, "What you'll need to do..."

10) Avoid chewing, eating, and drinking while on the telephone.

11) Avoid using slang when handling incoming telephone calls.

12) Be sure all messages you take are dated, that the time of the call is written on the message, and your initials or signature is at the bottom.

Wayne State College

ANSWERING A CALL

If you are asked to answer a call, please answer with, 1) *"Good Morning / Afternoon,"* 2) *"Wayne State College Library / (department you are in). This is (your name)."* Please refer to the page on Telephone Procedures for other suggestions on effective handling of telephone calls.

The library receives several types of calls. If...
* the caller wishes to speak to a person in the area, call that person to the telephone. State the callers name as you hand the person the telephone.

* the caller wishes to speak to a person who is not in the area at the time, you have several options.

    1)   Transfer the call to another telephone where the person wanted is available (see How to Transfer a Call).

    2)   Say, "He/She is away from his/her desk right now. May I take a message?" (NEVER say the person is "on break" or "at lunch." The library is run like any other business.)

          If the caller would like to leave a message, record all information ACCURATELY on a telephone message pad by the phone. Always repeat the spelling of the caller's name, the phone number, and the contents of the message. Be sure you have filled out the message correctly and fully, then sign your name at the bottom.

* if possible, try to resolve the callers need. Say, "_ name _ is not in the area at this time. May I help you?"

* the caller asks you to look for or page someone studying in the library, politely tell them that you may not leave the desk area to search the library, however, you can offer to leave a note on the message board. Be sensitive to the fact that a real emergency may necessitate looking for the person.

THE 1ST (NO PANIC) PERIODICAL SERVICES QUIZ!

PLEASE TAKE A FEW MINUTES TO ANSWER THESE QUESTIONS WHICH IDENTIFY ROUTINES THAT OCCUR ON THE JOB. THE PURPOSE OF THIS QUIZ IS FOR THE FULL-TIME STAFF TO DETERMINE WHICH AREAS OF OUR WORK NEED FURTHER INSTRUCTIONS OR TRAINING.

1. The phone rings. You answer it. What do you say?

ANSWER: Meader Library, Periodical Services.

---

2. You are straightening a newspaper room on April 1, 1994. The latest issue of the <u>Los Angeles Times</u> is March 21, 1994. Where do you put it? (Circle correct answer)

   (a) Previous month   ANSWER: Current Month. Current month is always the
   (b) Current month   latest issue received.

---

3. You are straightening periodical shelves and find the boxes out of order. Which box comes first? (Circle correct answer) Write where you would look to find correct order.

   (a) <u>The Journal of Taxation</u>   ANSWER: (a) taxation comes
   (b) <u>Journal of the American Taxation Association</u> before the American...
                                          Check the MLPL for correct order.

4. We get two copies of <u>The Pacific Business News.</u> Where do they go?

ANSWER: 1 copy stays on the 5th floor. The other gets routed.

---

5. Someone calls and asks who the governor of Hawaii was in 1957. What do you do?

ANSWER: Transfer the call to the Reference Desk.

---

6. A periodical returns with a routing slip and some of the initials are crossed off. "BV" remains. What do you do?

Route the periodical to Barbara Voigt in an inter-office mail envelope,

---

7. A patron comes to the service desk and wants to browse through a periodical on reserve. He doesn't know which date he needs and wants to look at all of that title on reserve. What do you do? (circle correct answer)

   (a) Let him go behind the counter to look at the reserves.
   (b) Take his ID and let him take all the reserves to a carrel.
   (c) Take his ID and have him sign out each issue (suggest that he look through a year at a time).
   (d) Take all of the reserve title to the service desk and wait until he finds the one he wants. Take his ID and have him sign out that issue.

ANSWER: (c). (d) would take too much of our time.

8. You are adding a bottle of toner to a Minolta printer and hear the bell at the service desk. You accidently spill toner on the edge of the hopper, the plastic pop-out tray and on the floor. What do you do?

ANSWER: The service desk always comes first.

Lebanon Valley College

STUDENT LIBRARY ASSISTANT TRAINING QUIZ

NAME_____

Please feel free to go to the specific areas and <u>check out</u> the answer first hand. The object is to make you feel comfortable with the job and to bring about top notch efficiency here in the library. Use this quiz to build your knowledge. At the end of training period you will be expected to take the test without the benefit of aid.

PROFESSORS' RESERVE MATERIAL

1. A professor comes in to put <u>class materials</u> on reserve. A form card must accompany the material. If he needs a form, where will you find one_____.

2. What do you do with the reserve material and the card?
   _____.

3. Do we have a regular reserve card (such as public libraries use) to reserve books for patrons as the books become available? _____.

4. If you can't find reserve material on shelf, what two things do you check?
   _____.

OVERDUE BOOKS

5. A book is due Sept. 15th. It comes back Sept. 20th. Figure the fine.
   FINE = _____.

6. A book is due Sept. 15th. It comes back Sept. 25th and they do not pay at the time it is returned. Figure the fine. FINE = _____.

7. A book is due Sept. 15th and is returned October 6th. The person wants to pay the fine immediately. Figure the fine. FINE = _____.

8. An overdue book incurs a _____ cent fine each day.

9. Are fines charged for the days when the library is closed? _____.

10. What four things do you do to the overdue list when an overdue book is returned?
    A._____
    B._____
    C._____
    D._____

11. What is the maximum fine per book? _____.

12.   Where will you find a pair of scissors?_____.

13.   A stapler?_____
      Staples?_____
      Scotch tape?_____
      Pencil sharpeners?_____

14.   What do you do with a book when you can't find the circulation card in the
      circulation file?_____.

15.   There are two types of overlays in the circulation file. What do the long overlays tell
      you?_____.

16.   What do the short overlays mean?_____.

17.   Four categories of library materials do not receive overlays. Name at least three.

      _____   _____   _____

      _____

18.   How are the cards in the circulation file filed?_____.

19.   What do you do when someone comes to the desk and asks to pick up ILL material
      that has come in?_____.

20.   Where is the ILL material kept?_____.

21.   Do you charge them anything for ILL materials?_____ have them sign out anything
      for ILL materials?_____.

22.   Where are the ILL request forms kept?_____.

23.   A call comes to the desk for Mr. Paustian. You look on the phone handle and see his
      extension number 6118. How would you transfer the call? The phone is ringing in
      the office and no one is picking up on it. You should retrieve the call at the desk
      rather than running to the office, but how do you retrieve that call to the desk phone?
      _____.
      Where can you find handy information about the phone system?_____
      _____.

24.   Which piece of information is essential in order to renew a book: author, title or call
      number?_____. How do you renew books?_____
      _____.

25.   Where do you put the renewed card?_____.

26.   Can you renew books over the phone?_____.

Lebanon Valley College

27. A community member (9th grade) wants a borrowers card. What do you do?
_____.

28. A community member (zip code 17104) wants a borrowers card. What do you do?
_____.

29. An area student from a nearby college wants to borrow books. What do you do?
_____.
How will you know which colleges have privileges?_____
_____. What is the time span
before this patron can check out materials?_____.
This "area student patron" wants to check out CD's and contemporaries, can he?
_____.

30. Suppose this "area student patron" does not go to a participating school. Is there
another way he might be able to check-out books?_____.

31. Where are community member applications kept?_____.

32. Can a REGULAR community member (not area student) who has just filled out the
application for a borrowers card 5 minutes ago take out books today? Explain your
answer._____
_____

33. Alarm #1 goes off. What do you do._____
_____.

34. Someone can't find a book on the shelves. What form can they fill out to request a
search?_____where it it found?_____
What do you do with it when it's filled out?_____.

35. Can compact discs leave library?_____. For how long?_____
Can CD Players leave the library?_____. For how long?_____
Can Reserve Material leave the library?_____.
For how long?_____explain_____
_____.

36. What 2 types of library materials do you keep ID for?_____
_____.

37. Someone has lost a set of keys. Where would you look for them?
_____.

38. How long do regular books circulate?_____.
CD's?_____Contemporary books?_____.

39. Where will you find "check-out" cards for faculty to check out the magazines? _____ How does that work? _____
   _____
   _____.
   Where do you file the card after they fill it out? _____.
   _____.
   Where will the professor put this magazine when he brings it back? _____
   _____. Who will tell him WHERE to return it
   to? _____. Can magazines circulate to students? _____

40. How do professors check out regular books? _____
   _____CDs_____Contemporaries_____

VIDEOS

41. Where are the "Library" videos kept? _____.
   Who is allowed to take them out overnight? _____.
   Who is allowed to use them "in house" only _____.
   Is the community borrower allowed to use videos "in house" _____.
   Do professors sometimes put "Library" videos on reserve? _____.
   Do professors sometimes put "personal" videos on reserve? _____.
   How will you know where to put the video when it comes back? Does it belong back
   in the video cabinet or on the reserve shelf? _____
   _____
   Where are "reserve videos" kept? _____.

COPIERS

42. How much are regular 8 1/2 x 11 size copies? _____
   8 1/2 x 14? _____   11 x 17? _____

43. How much are copies that are enlarged or reduced? _____
   Someone has 20 copies of the same original. Figure the cost _____.
   Someone request 2 copies of the same original - you will send them to the coin-op.
   Why? _____
   _____.
   Do we make copies for the public anymore? _____.

44. The coin-op is telling you to add paper. You look at it and determine that there is
   plenty of paper in it. What three things do you check?
   1.
   2.
   3.

Lebanon Valley College

Where can you find this information about what to check, in case you've forgotten?
_____.

MICROFILM COPIER (not the "beast" Microfilm copier at the desk)

45. What does P1 mean?_____.

46. What do you do when you see a small red flashing light?_____
_____.

47. If you can't remember what any of the **P** or **C** error messages mean, where would you look to find out?_____.

50. Where will you find the supplies for these two machines_____or_____.

CALL NUMBERS

48. Place the following "call numbers" in order.

B	B	B	B	B	B	B
656	655	665	665	655.1	655.1	655.1
.C6	.C63	.C472	.G47	.C59	.C59	.C595
G2	G3	A4		G2	G2	G2
					1980	

SECURITY SYSTEM

49. Which books leaving the library **must** be desensitized?_____.

50. If a FACULTY member signs out a magazine, do you desensitize it, or walk it around the gates?_____.

51. Do you desensitize software?_____, cassettes?_____, CD's_____,
Recordings (LP)?_____.

52. What do you do when the security system alarm goes off?_____
_____
_____

PERIODICAL WORKSHEET

Exercise 1

1. Use *ProQuest* to find an article dealing with "Baby Jessica" which appeared in 1993. Who wrote this article? When and where did it appear.

    Author _____ _____

    Periodical Title _____

    Volume_____Date_____Pages_____

    Use L-R's Periodicals holdings list to find out which years of this magazine the library includes:

    Years unbound _____

    Microfilm/microfiche (# and dates)_____

2. Use the *Newsbank Electronic Information System* to locate a December 7, 1990, newspaper article which reported that the Persian Gulf crisis will contribute to the budget deficit (see GOVERNMENT FINANCE, FEDERAL-budget deficits-attitudes and opinions). Record below the microfiche locator code for this article.

    Code_____ _____

    Find this article on the Newsbank microfiche and provide the following information:

    Author_____

    Title _____

    Newspaper title _____

3. Use the *ERIC* database to find a research done on gifted kindergarten students in North Carolina in the field of mathematics and science. Document the following information below:

    ERIC fiche number_____

    Author_____ Pages_____

SUPERVISION AND PERFORMANCE REVIEW

Supervision

Evaluation

Alfred University

We are interested in your candid opinions regarding your job (the training you have received, your perception of the work you are doing, and how the library staff supports, or does not support, you in your work). Your input will allow us to evaluate our management skills and our efforts in making your time spent at Herrick Memorial Library valuable.

1. How many semesters have you worked in the library?

2. What area(s) have you worked in?

3. Do you think you have been adequately trained for the job?

4. What do you like most about working in the library?

5. What do you like least about working in the library?

6. Do you feel a part of the overall library staff?

7. If you could change anything about your work in the library, what would you change?

8. Explain what you think the goals of the library are.

9. How do you think you help achieve these goals?

10. Do you think your supervisor or other members of the staff are concerned about your goals as a student and/or your goals beyond Alfred University?

11. Has this survey covered all your concerns?

12. How can we improve the "Evaluation of Student Assistant" form AND the "Evaluation by Student Assistant" form?

Please use reverse side if necessary.

FRINGE BENEFITS:

YES , there are some!

1. One week grace period before service charge on overdue books:

   If a book checked out to you is overdue, you will not have to pay a service charge for the first week, although you are still responsible for renewing it.

2. Study on the job if assigned tasks are completed:

   Circulation and Periodicals desk workers may do personal work during their work hours, _if assigned tasks are completed._

3. Flexible work hours:

   Some departments allow flexibility in scheduling work hours.

4. Improved research skills:

   On-the-job training will improve your ability to do library research for classes.

5. Improved interpersonal skills:

   Working at the public desks will enable you to sharpen interpersonal skills through contact with library users.

Dickinson College

Student employees are highly valued members of the library staff. Their contributions to the work of the various library departments are substantial and during large portions of the day the library is confidently -- and entirely -- left in their hands. In order to maintain the high quality of library staff and services, however, the library has had to establish the following minimum expectations of all of its student employees, no matter how long they have been employed nor in what capacity they serve. It is important for all students to familiarize themselves with these minimum standards at the beginning of the school year. Failure to meet them is a serious breach of a student's terms of employment and, in some cases, will be grounds for immediate dismissal.

1. Student employees are expected to conduct themselves and perform their work in a mature, responsible manner. Specifically:

    a. A job in the library is not an opportunity to study. Students working in public areas in particular are to remain alert to patron needs, concentrating first and foremost on their department responsibilities and on any extra tasks which they see need to be done or which they have been asked to do. An upright posture and friendly public manner should be maintained at all times, and students are asked to dress appropriately for their work, keeping in mind that they may be the first or only representatives of the library staff encountered by some library patrons. Because they must remain particularly aware of and sensitive to the environment around them, student employees are not permitted to use Walkmans or other personal listening equipment when at work.

    b. Personal conversations, except in an emergency, are not permitted either in-person or over the telephone. This includes conversations between student employees as well as between employees and friends who do not work in the library.

c. An atmosphere of quiet and order must be preserved in all areas of the library so that patrons are free to study undisturbed and so that employees may concentrate on their work. Necessary, work-related conversations should be conducted in quiet voices which do not carry into other areas.

d. Student employees must, of course, abide by all of the usual library regulations. This includes the rule that smoking, food and beverages are not allowed in the library. Any student found to be eating, drinking or smoking while on duty will be issued an automatic warning that any further violations of the library's regulations will result in immediate dismissal.

2. Library student employees must work their assigned hours during all times when the college is in session. This includes the entire Fall Pause period and the entire period between the last day of classes and 4:00 pm on the last scheduled day of exams. These rules apply to all students employed in all areas of the library.

Procedures for finding substitutes or, in some departments, arranging "make-up" hours when students cannot work at their originally scheduled times, are described in the Student Employee Handbook given to all students when they first begin working in the library. It should be noted, however, that "sub requests" are only a convenience designed to assist students who are trying to find other students to substitute for them. The mere posting of such a request does not absolve a student from responsibility for working as scheduled.

Failure to report to work without finding a substitute or contacting a supervisor for prior approval will result in an automatic warning to the student from the Chairman of the Department of Library Resources that a second occurrence anytime in the course of the year will result in immediate dismissal. Students repeatedly reporting to work more than a few minutes late without prior explanation and/or approval will be issued the same warning.

3. Student employees are under the general supervision of all members of the full time staff and also the student supervisors in the evenings and on weekends. This means that, while each student will have an immediate supervisor with whom to work out a specific schedule and set of responsibilities, he or she is also expected to respond promptly and courteously to requests from any student supervisor or any member of the full time staff.

Lenoir-Rhyne College

CARL A. RUDISILL LIBRARY
LATE EVENING SUPERVISOR CHECKSHEET

SUPERVISOR _____

DATE _____

Check the following problems encountered:

_____ Security didn't show up at closing

_____ Security didn't respond to call

_____ Had problems with patrons

Comments _____

_____

_____ Had problems with student assistants

Comments _____

_____

_____ Had problems with computer room students or personnel

Comments _____

_____

_____ Other problems

Comments _____

_____

_____ Nothing transpired

Signed _____

Leave this form on CBS desk.

<u>Welcome to Knight-Capron Library</u>

We are happy you have joined our staff as a student assistant. By working here, you will be helping our patrons utilize the library to its fullest extent. At the same time, you will be learning to use the library more effectively for your own studies.

Student assistants occupy an important position in the work of the library. When on duty, you represent the library to the faculty, the students, and the general public who use the library's resources. Our library is a service institution. Therefore, it is essential that we all respond to our patrons with courtesy, friendliness, and a helpful attitude.

To provide efficient service, you will need to know as much about the library as possible. Never hesitate to ask a library staff member about something that is not known to you.

Student duties are concerned only with Circulation Desk procedures and Stack operations. **YOU ARE NEVER EXPECTED TO OFFER REFERENCE ASSISTANCE.** All reference questions should be referred to the librarian on duty. Please do not give out information about which you are in doubt.

The following is a basic orientation to your job, our expectations of you, and explanations of various policies and procedures you need to know to perform your job well. This manual will help you successfully maintain efficiency. If you are unsure of procedures, please refer to this booklet or ask a supervisor. Remember, **NO QUESTION IS A STUPID QUESTION!!!**

All student assistants are expected to adhere to the guidelines set forth in this manual. If you fail to conform to these guidelines, you will be released from library employment and referred to the Financial Aid Office for other placement.

Please ask questions about any procedures you do not fully understand. You will be tested on certain standard procedures after undergoing a few weeks of training. Remember, **ASK QUESTIONS.**

Ona Turner
Circulation Supervisor
Revised 8/93

Library Info...

<u>Please discuss the following information with Jackie.</u>

***STUDENT ADVISOR - Lenora is a student advisor - so please send the student back to Technical Services when they are asking for their advisor.

***CURRICULUM CHECKOUT - When checking out boxes of Curriculum materials, please check the count on the outside of the box and make sure all items are in before it is checked out and also that all items are in when it is checked in. The box is barcoded.

***CHANGE - We DO NOT change $20.00 bills, please send them to the den or the bookstore. If they are paying a fine, then we do take the $20.00 bill.

***API - We do an API when a record is not found. This assigns the barcode to the appropriate student record. When doing this verify that they are a regular student and not a graduate student. DO NOT type in the expiration date - the computer does this.

***PPF - You can only do a PPF (pay patron fine) if the books have been returned. Use the DPF (display patron fines) to see what fines are final and can be paid.

***PAPER CHECKOUTS - Fill the form out completely when doing a paper checkout. Stamp the due date in the book and on the form. Use patron barcode on form.
If an item is returned and does not have a barcode, pull the paper checkout slip that goes to the book.

***MVF - MVF is for the music vertical file upstairs by the M's. MVF goes in the file cabinet, not on the shelves with the M's.

***RED TAPE - Please watch the back of books. Books with red tape (REFERENCE books) have been misshelved in the regular collection. Remember tape on the back of a book usually means that the book does not go on the regular shelves.

***ILL - Interlibrary Loan material with a green label instead of a pink label are like reserves. They can be used in the library only. So please take an ID and treat them just like reserves.

***VCR TAPES - If someone has to use the VCR tapes when the Media Center is not open, please have the reference librarian on duty let them into the viewing room.

***MONEY - Please count change carefully. If more change is needed please check with Jackie, Ethel, or the reference librarian.

SUBSTITUTION APPROVAL FORM

Student Responsible:_____ Today's Date:____

Signature:_____

Student Substituting for Above:_____

Signature:_____ Date:_____

Date & Time Slot to be Filled:_____

Supervisor's Signature:_____

Date:_____

SUBSTITUTION APPROVAL FORM

Student Responsible:_____ Today's Date:____

Signature:_____

Student Substituting for Above:_____

Signature:_____ Date:_____

Date & Time Slot to be Filled:_____

Supervisor's Signature:_____

Date:_____

Simpson College

Date/time	Accomplishments	Concerns

Student Log

OCCIDENTAL COLLEGE LIBRARY

<u>INTELLECTUAL FREEDOM POLICY</u>
<u>AND</u>
<u>RIGHT TO PRIVACY STATEMENT</u>

It is imperative for ethical, moral and legal reasons that we protect the privacy of all persons using library materials. Each person has the right to check out and use library materials without the fear of harrassment, pressure, or intimidation by someone else who needs the material or disapproves of it.

Librarian's must protect each user's right to privacy with respect to information sought or received, and materials consulted, borrowed, or acquired. Therefore, the following information is not to be revealed to anyone other than Occidental College librarians or library staff. It is not to be revealed to patrons, faculty, administrators, other students, police, credit bureaus, etc.:

1. Patrons names, addresses or telephone numbers.
2. Employees home addresses or telephone numbers.
3. The name of the person who has an item checked out whether the person is a student or an employee.
4. What items a person has checked out may be revealed only to the person him/herself.
5. A person's debts may be revealed only to the person him/herself. If a question is received by the Business or Registrar's office, refer the inquiry to a library staff member.
6. How the security system works.

Anyone seeking such information in spite of the library's policy, will be referred to the College Librarian, the College Administration, and ultimately, to the College's legal council, if necessary.

REFER ANY QUESTIONS ABOUT THIS POLICY TO A STAFF MEMBER.

As an employee of the Occidental College Library, I understand my obligation to support the above stated policies. I further understand that violation of these policies will be cause for dismissal.

_____
PRINT NAME

_____
SIGNATURE   DATE

Wayne State College

Workstudy Rights

GRIEVANCE

If you have a complaint or a problem with your job or your supervisor, request a meeting with your supervisor to discuss the problem.

If the issue is not resolved, request a meeting with the Director of Information Services and your supervisor to discuss it further. We hope that the problem can be resolved to everyone's satisfaction at or before this meeting.

If the issue still is not resolved, you may submit a written complaint to the Director of Information Services stating the problem, pertinent background information, and how you would like to see the problem resolved. Your supervisor then submits a similar document. If necessary, the Director of Information Services makes the final decision on any action to be taken.

DISCRIMINATION

Acts of discrimination based on race, sex, religion, handicaps, age, or national origin are prohibited by law.

If you feel you have been discriminated against, please follow the grievance procedures described above.

Date: January 15, 1994

STUDENT EMPLOYEE EVALUATION

STUDENT'S NAME   Jennifer xxxxxxxxxxxxxxxxxxx
NUMBER OF SEMESTERS WORKED IN SCIENCE LIBRARY 1

MAJOR RESPONSIBILITIES

PUBLIC SERVICE/CIRCULATION
Circulation desk duties include the circulation of library
materials including reserve materials with proper consideration
for library policy, courtesy to patrons, and efficiency.

*Comments: Jennifer has been very quick to learn about her duties
at the circulation desk. She serves patrons eagerly and
efficiently.*

PUBLIC SERVICE/ASSISTANCE IN THE LIBRARY
Helping patrons in the library includes assisting in the location
of materials, use of microform machines, photocopy machines, and
general direction to reference materials or referral to a
reference librarian as needed. Also included is assistance with
interlibrary loan forms and photocopy requests.

*Comments: Jennifer is extremely gracious and able. She assists
in any situation with which she is familiar, and asks for help if
she needs something which is not apparently available.*

LIBRARY ORGANIZATION
Library organization includes prompt placement of library
materials in their correct locations. Shelving of all library
materials in a timely manner insures that patrons can easily
locate needed items. Library organization also includes
completion of necessary paperwork for statistical reports, making
sure patron request forms are placed appropriately for further
action, notifying regular staff of situations requiring their
attention.

*Comments: Jennifer begins her work immediately and tends to all
routine duties without supervision. She pays attention to detail
and does a thorough job.*

Colgate University

GENERAL LIBRARY MAINTENANCE
General library maintenance includes opening and closing the
library on schedule and following the protocol for doing so.
Closing and opening doors and windows as needed, picking up
litter arranging chairs, calling a regular staff member or the
security officer as needed to deal with disturbances, and
otherwise generally enforcing rules regarding quiet, not allowing
food, etc.

Comments: Jennifer tends to these tasks without supervision.

PERSONAL WORK ETHIC
Personal work ethic includes following all guidelines for
attendance/substitutions, punctuality, courtesy to patrons and
library staff. It includes correct and timely preparation of
work schedules, time sheets and pay vouchers, and other written
and verbal communications regarding the same. Ability to work
with minimum supervision, learning routines, paying attention to
detail, thoroughness and completion of assigned tasks, and
willingness all contribute to the personal work ethic.

Comments: Jennifer is dependable, apt, careful and thorough.
She learns quickly and is extremely responsible. She has never
failed to act appropriately. She finds a substitute when
necessary, and volunteers to substitute when others have
requests. Jennifer exercises good judgement, communicating
requests for help in problem solving at appropriate times. I hope
that Jennifer will continue to work for the science library for
as many semesters as she is on campus. Jennifer's pleasant
demeanor endears her to staff and patrons alike. The only thing
that could improve her performance is experience.

_____
Carol Compton
Supervisor of Student Employees

Please sign this form and return it to me. I will provide you
with a copy. Also, please add your comments in the space below.
If, as you read over this evaluation you recall questions you
might have about a procedure, or anything else which seems
lacking in your training, please let me know.

_____
Jennifer xxxxxxxxxxxx
_____Date

122 - Supervision and Performance Review

Gustavus Adolphus College

ANNUAL STUDENT ASSISTANT EVALUATION

Folke Bernadotte Memorial Library
Gustavus Adolphus College

Name _____   I.D. # _____

Department _____   Class _____

Job description or title _____   Time in position _____

INSTRUCTIONS

STUDENT   On the back of this form, complete self-rating for each criterion by placing a check mark on the **left** side of the column in each of the ranking categories (commendable, satisfactory, etc.)

SUPERVISOR   Evaluate each student assistant using the criteria shown by placing a check mark on the **right** side of the appropriate column. If the characteristic does not apply or if you do not have sufficient information, check the *Not Applicable* column.

SUPERVISOR'S COMMENTS: _____

_____

_____

_____

_____

_____

GOAL SETTING: (if applicable) _____

_____

_____   _____
    Signature of Supervisor   - *Date*

STUDENT'S COMMENTS: (complete after interview) _____

_____

_____

_____

_____   _____
    Signature or Student   *Date*

Gustavus Adolphus College

Criteria   Ranking Categories

	COMMENDABLE	SATISFACTORY	NEEDS IMPROVEMENT	N/A
Dependability *Punctual, reliable, responsible; observes attendance policy.*				
Quality of Work *Demonstrates knowledge and skills essential for work. Accurate, thorough, uses time economically.*				
Quantity of Work *Performs expected/assigned amount of work; works well under pressure.*				
Attitude Toward Work *Interested; willing to work at difficult or disagreeable tasks; takes instruction willingly.*				
Initiative *Performs assigned tasks without prompting; performs unassigned work.*				
Leadership *Influences and inspires others by example to do better work.*				
Cooperation *Courteous, friendly; works well with others; conscious of responsibility to working group.*				
Judgement *Shows self-control; makes sound decisions; uses common sense.*				
Personal Appearance *Neat, suitably dressed; complies with dress code where applicable.*				

Note: This information will be on record in the Library Administration Office
and the college's Financial Aid Office.

Southwest State University

1992-93/STUDENT EMPLOYEE EVALUATION REPORT

_____	_____/____/_____	_____
Name of Employee	Social Security#	Year in School

Describe the duties and responsibilities of this employee._____

_____

_____

4-OUTSTANDING 3-ABOVE AVERAGE 2-AVERAGE 1-BELOW AVERAGE N.E.-NO EVALUATION
IF A CATEGORY CANNOT BE RATED OBJECTIVELY, PLEASE MARK THE "NO EVALUATION"
BOX.

PLEASE CHECK APPROPRIATE BOX

	4	3	2	1	N.E.
Knowledge of LC Classification system: Able to shelve with few mistakes or problems.					
Shelving speed: Able to shelve quickly and accurately.					
Rewanding of books: Wand books before taking to 5th floor, if necessary.					
Book drops: Regularly checking book drops & reshelving books.					
Process for damaged books: Know what to do with books needing repair.					
Inventory Wander: Ability to put in codes, work quickly and accurately.					
Fix shelving errors: Ability to find and fix any shelving errors as we see them.					
Self motivated: Ability to find things to do if there are no books on the shelves.					
Ability to work alone: Can do the work and not goof off while on Library time.					
Book searches: Ability to find books that patrons cannot.					
_____					
_____					
_____					

Transylvania University

MID-YEAR EVALUATION OF LIBRARY ASSISTANT

Name of Student _____ Name of Supervisor _____

Areas of Strength

Areas for Improvement

Plans for Improvement/Enrichment

_____   _____
Supervisor's Signature   Date

Student's Comments

_____   _____
Student's Signature   Date

126 - Supervision and Performance Review

Transylvania University

WORK-STUDY STUDENT EVALUATION SHEET

Student's Name _____ Position _____

Period of time student has been in present position: From _____ to _____

Evaluator's Name _____ Department _____

In each section, put a check mark next to the response which, in your opinion, most closely describes this student's work performance. If you wish, use the space marked "Additional Comments" to explain your rating of any or all the factors. Please discuss this evaluation with the student, as this rating will be used in assigning positions for the coming academic year. Please return this form to the Office of Student Aid, 304 Old Morrison, by June 1.

1. QUALITY OF WORK:
   _____ Work slip-shod, usually untidy about work habits
   _____ Work barely passable; errors frequent
   _____ Average quality work; makes occasional errors; usually neat
   _____ Work of good quality; errors uncommon
   _____ Exceptionally neat and accurate; superior quality

2. QUANTITY OF WORK:
   _____ Output consistently below regular standards
   _____ Works slowly; rather low production
   _____ Completes average amount of work
   _____ Good productivity; volume of work more than satisfactory
   _____ Consistently completes an exceptional amount of work

3. RELIABILITY:
   _____ Totally unreliable
   _____ Marginal reliability; requires occasional checking on routine tasks
   _____ Usually can be depended upon but must be checked on more important matters
   _____ Dependable; rarely requires follow-up once instructions are given
   _____ Can be relied upon completely; merits utmost confidence

4. ATTITUDE:
   _____ No interest in job; cooperates only when forced to
   _____ Marginal interest; occasionally uncooperative or unpleasant
   _____ Good interest in work; usually cooperative and pleasant
   _____ Above average interest in work; meets others halfway; accepts suggestions without resentment
   _____ Superior interest in work; constructive attitude

5. PUNCTUALITY AND ATTENDANCE:
   _____ Completely undependable; often absent or late; does not call employer.
   _____ Undependable; may be late or absent without good reason; does not notify employer
   _____ Dependable; may be late on occasion; notifies employer if unable to report
   _____ Very dependable; has legitimate excuse when absent or late; notifies employer
   _____ Totally dependable; absent or late only when unavoidable; notifies employer in advance when unable to report

Supervision and Performance Review - 127

Transylvania University

6. OVERALL EVALUATION (Please rate the student on overall performance)

_____ Unsatisfactory
_____ Below average (has potential to improve)
_____ Satisfactory (meets normal requirements)
_____ Above average
_____ Excellent

7. Would you like to retain this student for work next year? ____ yes ____ no
   If no, please state reason. _____
   _____

8. Did this student receive some on-the-job training, which you felt was adequate,
   to improve his/her skills and performance? ____ yes ____ no.

Additional Comments:

_____

_____

_____

_____

Please discuss this evaluation with the student. It is hoped that the work-study
experience has been profitable, educational, and enjoyable to the student while
satisfying basic employment needs of the institution. A lack of communication can
be a source of displeasure between the student and the employer.

This evaluation was discussed with me. _____
                                              (employee's signature)

Evaluator's Signature _____ Date _____

Interim Report:

University of Wisconsin - Superior

Jim Dan Hill Library
Student Employee Evaluation

Student's Name_____	Job Title_____	Evaluation:
Identification Number_____		Probation___
Dates of Employment_____	Work Study__	Annual __
_____	Student Assistant__	Final __
	Other__	Other __

PERFORMANCE RATINGS

EXCELLENT	E	Performance levels exceptional and outstanding
VERY GOOD	VG	Consistently exceeds performance levels
GOOD	G	Consistently meets the performance levels
NEEDS IMPROVEMENT	NI	Does not consistently meet the performance levels
UNSATISFACTORY	U	Performance unacceptable, immediate corrective action required
N/A	N/A	Not applicable

Performance Levels (see attached departmental - job description)

		E	VG	G	NI	U	N/A
ADAPTABILITY	Adjusts readily to changes in job duties; copes well with unanticipated and/or difficult situations; is open to suggestions about improving job performance.						
ATTENDANCE	punctual; adheres to work schedule, observes attendance policy.						
ATTITUDE	conscientious; enthusiastic; willing to do any task assigned; takes instructions willingly.						
COMMUNICATION SKILLS	follows both written and oral instructions; communicates clearly, both orally and in writing; listens carefully; gives good feedback.						
INITIATIVE	self-starter; suggests ideas for improving procedures; identifies and reports job-related problems; needs no follow up.						
INTERACTION	relates well with others; is cooperative with fellow employees; displays a courteous and helpful attitude with patrons and staff.						
JOB KNOWLEDGE	understands and demonstrates conceptual and technical aspects of the work.						

University of Wisconsin - Superior

		E	VG	G	NI	U	N/A
JUDGEMENT	utilizes job knowledge in decision-making; makes sound decisions; knows when to seek assistance; exercises common sense						
PRODUCTIVITY	accommodates normal work flow; volume and rate of work meet departmental job duties; efficiently uses time.						
QUALITY OF WORK	performs tasks neatly, accurately, thoroughly; attends to details, uses materials and time wisely.						
RESPONSIBILITY	works with minimum supervision; accountable for his/her work.						

POLICY COMPLIANCE Observes policies and procedures in the Jim Dan Hill Library Student Employee Handbook.

_____YES _____NO

If no, indicate problem and desired correction (see Supervisor's comments.)

This form is intended to serve as a catalyst for communication between the student and the supervisor relative to the job performed. Both the student and the supervisor are encouraged to add written comments BEFORE the document is signed. THIS INFORMATION IS CONFIDENTIAL AND IS RETAINED IN THE LIBRARY ADMINISTRATION OFFICE AND THE FINANCIAL AID OFFICE.

SUPERVISOR'S COMMENTS:

STUDENT'S COMMENTS:

_____   _____
Supervisor's Signature   Date   Student's Signature*   Date

*PLEASE NOTE: Your signature indicates that you have read this evaluation and discussed it with your supervisor.

130 - Supervision and Performance Review